delicious. ABC

Home Cooking

ABC

delicious.

Home Cooking

VALLI LITTLE

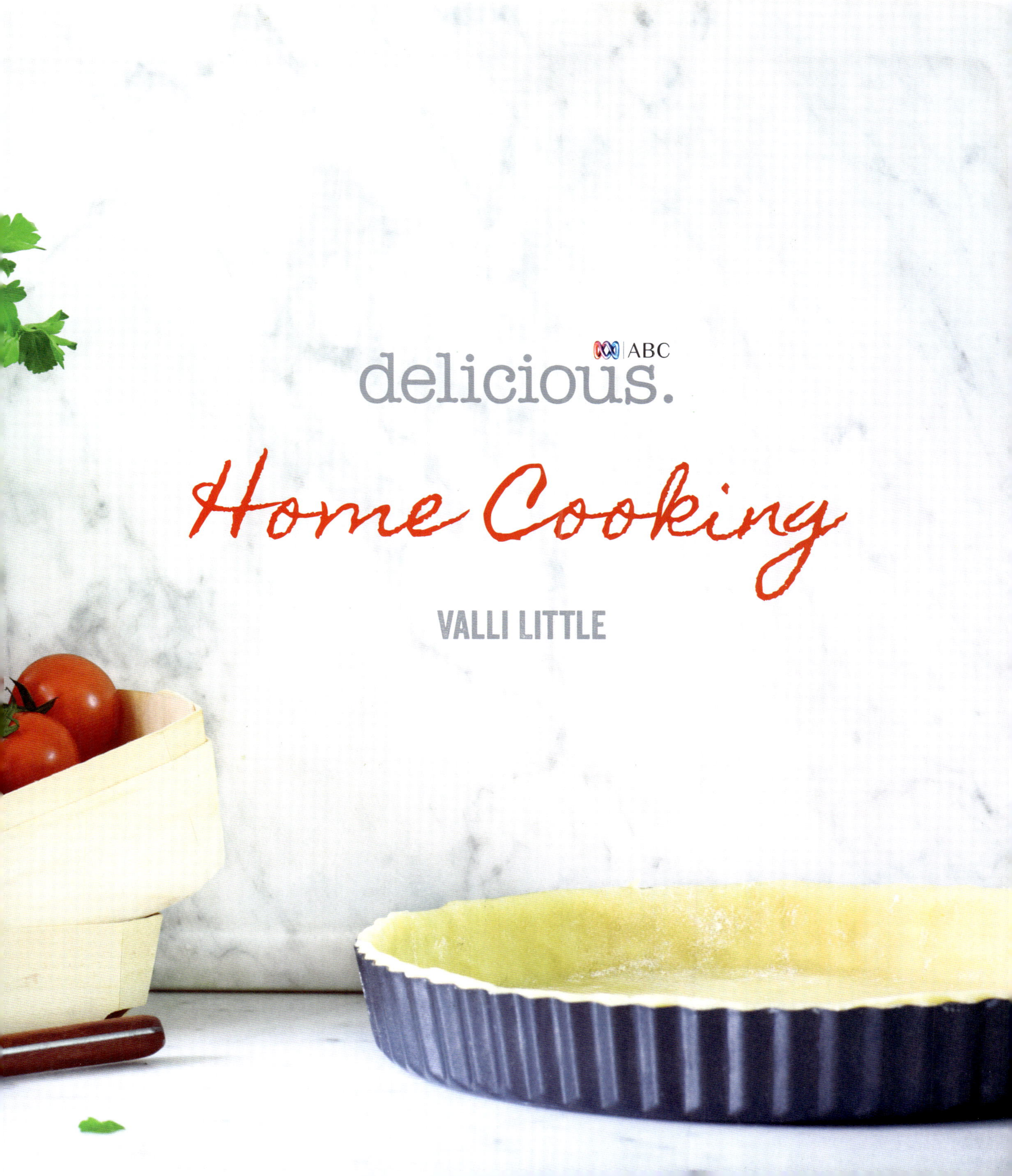

WELCOME

I ALWAYS REFER TO MYSELF as a cook, not a chef. Even though I was formally trained, I truly believe that the best recipes are learned in the kitchen rather than the classroom. Sourcing, cooking, tasting and sharing food is one of life's great pleasures, which is why some of our happiest memories (at least in my case) are made at the table.

So for my new book, I wanted to focus on home cooking, a subject dear to my heart. In my family, especially with two grown-up sons, a great deal of thought and effort was and still is required to come up with something different for dinner every night.

You won't find fancy restaurant-style dishes in here – it's all about recipes that reflect the sort of food I like to cook at home, whether it's a midweek meal for the family or something more impressive for the weekend when entertaining friends.

I am heartened by the fact that Australians seem to be moving on from the era of fast food and TV dinners, and finding joy in those special sights, smells and tastes that can only come from a home-cooked meal. It's great to see that visiting the local farmers' market is becoming a favourite weekend pastime for many people.

I hope that by inviting me into your kitchen with this book, we can work together to create some memorable meals for you to share at the table with your loved ones. So put on your apron, pick up that spoon, and let's get cooking!

Valli

Contents

File under Drinks

Sunkist Lemonad

1   cup Sunkist Lemon Juic
½ to 1 cup sugar
6   cups cold water

MIX ingredients
Amount   Method:

in season

apricots asparagus bananas
beans (butter, green) berries (blackberr
blueberry, boysenberry, strawberry)
capsicums cherries corn eggplants
mangoes nectarines peaches tomatoes zucch

SUMMER

CHILLED PEA SOUP WITH WASABI CREAM

30g unsalted butter
1 onion, finely chopped
1 pontiac potato (about 200g),
    peeled, chopped
2$^1/_2$ cups (625ml) chicken
    or vegetable stock
2 cups fresh or frozen peas
250g creme fraiche
1 tsp wasabi paste*
Wasabi peas* and chervil
    or mint leaves, to serve

Melt the butter in a saucepan over medium-low heat. Add the onion and cook, stirring, for 1-2 minutes until softened. Add the potato and stock, bring to a simmer over medium-high heat, then cook for 10 minutes, adding the fresh peas for the final 5 minutes of cooking time (3 minutes if frozen) or until tender. Use a stick blender to puree the soup until smooth. (Alternatively, allow to cool slightly, then puree in batches in a blender.) Season, then stir in half the creme fraiche. Chill for 1 hour.

Place the wasabi and remaining creme fraiche in a bowl, stirring to combine.

If necessary, adjust the consistency of the soup with a little water, then ladle soup into bowls or serving glasses, scatter with a few wasabi peas and top with a dollop of wasabi cream. Serve garnished with chervil or mint leaves. **Serves 4**

* From Asian food shops and selected supermarkets.

PRAWN, WHITE BEAN & CHORIZO SALAD

1 tbs olive oil

250g chorizo, sliced

12 green prawns, peeled (tails intact), deveined

400g can cannellini beans, rinsed, drained

250g punnet cherry tomatoes, halved

$1/2$ red onion, thinly sliced

1 cup flat-leaf parsley leaves, torn

$1/2$ cup mint leaves, torn

Dressing

1 garlic clove, crushed

1 tbs sherry vinegar or red wine vinegar

$1/3$ cup (80ml) extra virgin olive oil

Place the olive oil in a frypan over medium-high heat. Add the chorizo and cook, turning, for 2-3 minutes until crisp. Remove from the pan with a slotted spoon and drain on paper towel.

Add the prawns to the same frypan and cook for 1-2 minutes each side until just cooked. Set aside.

For the dressing, place all the ingredients in a bowl, season, then whisk to combine.

Place the beans, tomatoes, onion, parsley, mint, chorizo and prawns in large bowl. Add the dressing and toss to combine, then serve warm. **Serves 4**

BOMBAY SLIDERS

Sliders (mini burgers) are popping up on restaurant menus everywhere. They're also a fun idea when you're entertaining at home, especially at a cocktail party or summer barbecue.

500g chicken mince
$1/4$ cup chopped coriander
  leaves, plus extra leaves
  to serve
$1/4$ cup finely chopped
  spring onion
1 tsp ground cumin
1 small red chilli, seeds
  removed, chopped
2cm piece ginger, grated
$3/4$ cup (225g) whole-egg
  mayonnaise
2 tbs mild curry powder
1 tbs tomato sauce (ketchup)
1 tbs thick Greek-style
  yoghurt
1 garlic clove, crushed
2 tbs olive oil
12 small brioche or mini
  burger buns*, split, toasted
Mango chutney and micro
  salad leaves (optional),
  to serve

Place the chicken mince, coriander, spring onion, cumin, chilli, ginger, $1/4$ cup (75g) mayonnaise and $1^1/2$ tablespoons curry powder in a bowl. Mix well to combine, season, then shape into 12 small patties. Chill for 30 minutes to firm up.

Place the tomato sauce, yoghurt, garlic, and remaining $1/2$ cup (150g) mayonnaise and 2 teaspoons curry powder in a bowl. Season, then stir to combine. Set aside.

Place the oil in a frypan over medium-high heat. In batches, cook the patties for 2-3 minutes each side or until cooked through.

To serve, spread the base of each bun with some mango chutney, then top with the chicken patties, curry mayonnaise, extra coriander and micro salad leaves, if desired. Sandwich with the bun tops and secure with toothpicks or small skewers. **Makes 12**

* Order mini burger buns from bakeries.

KATAIFI PRAWNS WITH GREEN MANGO SALAD

This recipe is inspired by a dish from Ben O'Donoghue. Kataifi pastry is very finely shredded filo which is usually used in Greek desserts, but also works well in savoury dishes. I love the combination of the crunchy kataifi-wrapped prawns and a crisp salad.

¼ cup (35g) cornflour
1 eggwhite
150g kataifi pastry*
12 large green prawns, peeled
   (tails intact), deveined
Sunflower oil, to deep-fry

Green mango salad

2 green mangoes*,
   thinly shredded
2 Lebanese cucumbers, sliced
1 long red chilli, seeds
   removed, thinly sliced
1 cup coriander sprigs
1 cup mint sprigs
Juice of 1 lime, plus
   lime wedges to serve
1 tbs fish sauce
1 tbs brown sugar

Place the cornflour in a bowl and season. Lightly whisk the eggwhite in a separate bowl until frothy. Pull the kataifi strands apart into 12 sections, place on a work surface and cover with a damp tea towel.

Dip the prawns first in cornflour, shaking off any excess, then in the eggwhite. Wrap a kataifi pastry section around each prawn, keeping the remaining pastry covered with the tea towel as you work.

Half-fill a large saucepan or deep fryer with the oil and heat to 190°C (if you don't have a kitchen thermometer, a cube of bread dropped into the oil will turn golden after 30 seconds when the oil is hot enough). In batches, deep-fry the prawns for 2-3 minutes until golden. Drain on paper towel.

Meanwhile, for the green mango salad, place the green mango, cucumber, chilli and herbs in a large bowl. Whisk the lime juice, fish sauce and brown sugar together in a separate bowl, then drizzle over the salad and toss to combine.

Serve the kataifi prawns with the green mango salad and lime wedges. **Serves 4**

* Kataifi pastry is from Greek delis. Green mangoes are from Asian food shops and selected greengrocers.

TOMATO, GOAT'S CHEESE & POPPYSEED TARTINES

250g punnet vine-ripened
  cherry tomatoes
2 garlic cloves
1 tsp chopped tarragon
1 tsp brown sugar
1 tbs balsamic vinegar
1/4 cup (60ml) olive oil,
  plus extra to brush
120g soft goat's cheese
1 tbs milk
1 tbs poppyseeds
4 sourdough bread slices
Mint leaves, to serve

Preheat the oven to 160°C.

Divide the tomatoes into 4 bunches and place on a baking tray. Slice 1 garlic clove and place in a bowl with the tarragon, sugar, vinegar and oil, then whisk to combine. Season, then drizzle over the tomatoes. Roast for 30 minutes or until the tomatoes are soft and starting to split.

Meanwhile, place the goat's cheese, milk and poppyseeds in a bowl, season well and stir to combine. Set aside.

Preheat a barbecue or chargrill pan over high heat.

Brush the bread with oil, then grill for 1-2 minutes each side until charred. Halve the remaining garlic clove, then rub bread with the cut side of the garlic.

Spread the bread with the goat's cheese mixture and top with the tomatoes. Drizzle over the tomato roasting juices and serve garnished with mint.

Serves 4

GINGER & CHILLI KINGFISH CEVICHE

This dish is a bit of a fusion of cuisines. I've added fresh ginger to give an Asian twist to a South American favourite.

300g sashimi-grade hiramasa
   kingfish*
1/2 red onion, thinly sliced
1/2 cup (125ml) lime juice
   (from about 3 limes)
1 garlic clove, crushed
1cm piece ginger, grated
1 long green chilli, seeds
   removed, finely chopped
3 coriander stems,
   finely chopped
Micro herbs or coriander
   leaves and unsprayed edible
   flowers* (optional), to serve

Enclose the fish in plastic wrap and freeze for 20 minutes (this will make it easier to slice).

Meanwhile, soak the onion slices in a bowl of cold water for 10 minutes. Drain, then pat dry with paper towel. Set aside.

Place the lime juice, garlic, ginger, chilli and coriander stems in a small bowl. Season, then whisk to combine.

Unwrap the fish, then very thinly slice and arrange on serving plates. Drizzle with the lime dressing, then scatter over the onion. Serve garnished with herbs and edible flowers, if desired.

Serves 6

* Sashimi-grade hiramasa kingfish is available from fishmongers. Edible flowers are available from farmers' markets and selected greengrocers.

POTTED TROUT WITH DILL CUCUMBERS

These individual pots of spiced, hot-smoked trout are great for picnics.
They will keep in the fridge for up to 5 days.

250g hot-smoked trout,
   skin and bones removed
100g unsalted butter, softened,
   plus extra clarified butter
   to cover (see Extras, p 246)
1/2 tsp ground nutmeg
1/2 tsp ground mace*
   (optional)
1 tsp wholegrain mustard
Juice of 1 lemon
2 tbs chopped dill
Sliced baguette, to serve

Dill cucumbers

500g baby cucumbers (qukes)*
   or 4 small Lebanese
   cucumbers, thinly sliced
1 cup (250ml) white wine
1 cup (250ml) rice vinegar
250g caster sugar
6 dill sprigs
2 star anise
2 cloves
1/4 tsp coriander seeds

For the dill cucumbers, place the cucumbers in a colander in the sink and liberally sprinkle with salt. Allow to drain for 30 minutes, then rinse well and place in a bowl. Place the remaining ingredients in a saucepan and bring to a simmer over medium heat, stirring until the sugar dissolves. Pour over the cucumbers and stand for at least 1 hour to pickle.

Place the trout, softened butter, spices, mustard, lemon juice and dill in a food processor, season, then whiz until you have a coarse pâté. Spoon into four 1/2 cup (125ml) ramekins or pots and cover with clarified butter. Chill for at least 30 minutes or until set. Remove from the fridge 30 minutes before serving.

Bring the potted trout back to room temperature, then serve with the drained dill cucumbers and baguette slices. **Serves 4**

* Mace is the lacy outer layer that covers the nutmeg seed, available from selected delis and Herbie's Spices (herbies.com.au). Baby cucumbers are available in season from greengrocers.

LITTLE SEAFOOD TARTS

1 quantity parmesan pastry
  (see Extras, p 246) or use
  3 frozen, thawed shortcrust
  pastry sheets
2 avocados, chopped, tossed
  with a little lemon juice
16 cooked prawns, peeled,
  deveined
300g fresh cooked
  crabmeat*
Sweet paprika and
  wild rocket, to serve

Seafood sauce
1 egg
Dash of Tabasco
1 tbs Dijon mustard
2 tbs Worcestershire sauce
$1/3$ cup (80ml) tomato sauce
  (ketchup)
Juice of 1 lemon
2 cups (500ml) grapeseed oil

Preheat the oven to 180°C and grease six 12cm loose-bottomed tart pans.

Roll out the pastry to 5mm thick if using homemade. Use the pastry to line the tart pans, trimming the excess. Chill for 10 minutes.

Line the tart shells with baking paper and fill with pastry weights or uncooked rice, then bake for 10 minutes. Remove the paper and weights, then bake for a further 3-4 minutes until golden and dry. Allow to cool completely.

Meanwhile, for the seafood sauce, place the egg, Tabasco, mustard, Worcestershire, tomato sauce and lemon juice in a small food processor and whiz to combine. With the motor running, add the oil in a slow, steady stream until you have a thick sauce. Loosen with a little warm water, if necessary.

Filled the cooled tart shells with the avocado, prawns and crab, then drizzle with the seafood sauce and dust with a little sweet paprika. Serve the tarts garnished with wild rocket. **Serves 6**

* Available from fishmongers.

STRAWBERRY GAZPACHO

Sweet, ruby-hued strawberries are a natural choice for desserts, but that doesn't mean they should always be saved for the end of the meal. Try using them in this gazpacho with a difference.

2 x 250g punnets
  strawberries, hulled
1 garlic clove, chopped
1/2 onion, chopped
1/2 red capsicum, chopped
2 Lebanese cucumbers, seeds
  removed, chopped
1 small bunch tarragon
1/4 cup (60ml) balsamic vinegar
1/2 cup (125ml) extra virgin
  olive oil, plus extra to serve
1 cup (250ml) tomato juice
Thinly sliced jamon or
  prosciutto, croutons and
  unsprayed edible flowers*
  (optional), to serve

Reserve 2 strawberries for garnish. Place the remaining strawberries in a glass or ceramic bowl with the garlic, onion, capsicum, cucumber, tarragon, vinegar and oil, then roughly crush with a fork or potato masher. Cover and stand for 2-3 hours to allow the flavours to develop.

Use a stick blender to puree the strawberry mixture until smooth. (Alternatively, puree in batches in a blender.) Pass the soup through a sieve into a clean bowl, pressing down with the back of a spoon to extract as much juice as possible and discarding the solids. Stir in the tomato juice, then season. Chill the soup for at least 30 minutes.

Finely chop the reserved 2 strawberries. Ladle the chilled soup into bowls, top with the jamon or prosciutto and drizzle with extra oil. Serve garnished with the chopped strawberries, croutons and edible flowers, if desired. **Serves 4**

* From farmers' markets and selected greengrocers.

MEXICAN CORN CAKES WITH AVOCADO AND PRAWNS

2 avocados, chopped
2 tbs lime juice, plus
  lime wedges to serve
2 tbs sour cream
1/2 cup chopped coriander
  leaves, plus extra
  coriander leaves to serve
2 tsp ground cumin
2 jalapeno chillies, seeds
  removed, chopped,
  plus extra sliced jalapeno
  chilli to serve
1 cup (150g) plain flour
1 tsp baking powder
1 tbs caster sugar
2 eggs
1/2 cup (125ml) milk
2 cups (320g) corn kernels
  (from about 3 corn cobs)
1/2 cup thinly sliced
  spring onion
2 tbs olive oil
20 cooked prawns, peeled
  (tails intact), deveined

Place the avocado, lime juice, sour cream, 1/4 cup coriander, 1 teaspoon cumin and half the chilli in a food processor and whiz to a coarse paste. Set aside.

Sift the flour and baking powder into a bowl. Add the sugar, remaining 1 teaspoon cumin and a pinch of salt.

Place the eggs and milk in a separate bowl and lightly whisk to combine. Add the milk mixture to the flour mixture, whisking until you have a smooth, stiff batter. Add corn, spring onion, and remaining chilli and chopped coriander. Season, then stir to combine.

Place the oil in a non-stick frypan over medium-high heat. In batches, drop 2 tablespoons batter into the frypan for each corn cake and cook for 1-2 minutes each side until golden and cooked through. Drain on paper towel and keep warm while you cook the remaining corn cakes.

Divide the corn cakes among plates, then top with avocado puree, prawns, sliced jalapeno and extra coriander. Serve with lime wedges. **Serves 4**

TAGLIATELLE WITH CHEAT'S MEATBALLS AND CHERRY TOMATOES

If you don't have time to make the sauce, use a 600g jar good-quality pasta sauce instead.

600g pork & herb sausages,
  casings removed
1 tbs olive oil
250g punnet cherry tomatoes,
  halved
1/4 cup basil leaves, finely
  chopped, plus extra basil
  leaves to serve
400g tagliatelle or
  other long pasta
1/2 cup (40g) finely
  grated parmesan

Pasta sauce

1.5kg vine-ripened tomatoes
1/4 cup (60ml) extra virgin
  olive oil
2 garlic cloves, finely chopped
1 basil sprig
Pinch of caster sugar

For the pasta sauce, cut a cross in the base of each tomato and place in a large bowl. Pour over enough boiling water to cover, then stand for 30 seconds. Drain, then refresh immediately in a bowl of iced water. Once cool enough to handle, carefully peel, then cut into quarters, discarding the cores and seeds. Place the oil in a saucepan over medium-low heat. Cook the garlic, stirring, for 30 seconds or until fragrant, then add the tomato, basil sprig and sugar. Reduce heat to low, then simmer, stirring occasionally, for 30-40 minutes until the tomatoes have broken down and sauce is thick. Remove basil and season.

Meanwhile, roll the sausage meat into 3cm balls, then chill for 30 minutes to firm up.

Place the oil in a deep frypan over medium heat. Cook the meatballs, turning, for 3-4 minutes until browned. Add the pasta sauce and tomatoes, season, then reduce heat to low and simmer for 5-6 minutes until sauce is slightly reduced and the meatballs are cooked through. Stir through the chopped basil.

Meanwhile, cook the pasta according to the packet instructions until al dente. Drain, then add to the sauce and toss well to combine.

Divide the pasta and meatballs among shallow bowls. Sprinkle over the parmesan, then serve garnished with basil leaves. **Serves 4**

MACADAMIA-CRUMBED CHICKEN STRIPS

Crumbed chicken strips are classic finger food and this grown-up version uses macadamias to add a delicious, creamy crunch.

½ cup (75g) macadamias, roughly chopped
2 cups (100g) panko breadcrumbs*
1 cup (150g) plain flour
2 eggs, lightly beaten
12 chicken tenderloins or 4 x 170g chicken breast fillets, cut into thirds lengthways
Sunflower oil, to deep-fry

Tomato salsa
4 tomatoes, seeds removed, chopped
1 red onion, chopped
1 long green chilli, seeds removed, chopped
1 tbs grated ginger
2 tbs chopped coriander, plus extra leaves to serve
Juice of 1 lime, plus lime wedges to serve
⅓ cup (80ml) extra virgin olive oil

For the tomato salsa, place all the ingredients in a bowl, season, then toss to combine. Set aside.

Place the macadamias and breadcrumbs in a food processor and whiz to fine crumbs. Transfer to a bowl.

Place the flour in a separate bowl and season. Place the egg in a third bowl.

Dip the chicken first in flour, shaking off the excess, then in the egg and finally in the macadamia crumbs, making sure each piece is well coated. Chill for 20 minutes to firm up.

Preheat the oven to 150°C.

Half-fill a large saucepan or deep-fryer with the oil and heat to 190°C (if you don't have a kitchen thermometer, a cube of bread dropped into the oil will turn golden after 30 seconds when the oil is hot enough). In batches, deep-fry the crumbed chicken strips for 3-4 minutes until golden and cooked through. Remove with a slotted spoon and drain on paper towel. Transfer to a baking tray and keep warm in the oven while you cook the remaining chicken.

Serve the chicken strips with the tomato salsa, lime wedges and extra coriander leaves. **Serves 4**

* Available from supermarkets and Asian food shops; substitute dried breadcrumbs.

BLACKENED SALMON WITH PAPAYA MOJO

This papaya mojo is a Caribbean-inspired salsa that adds a cooling note to the spicy salmon. You can also make this dish with ocean trout.

1 tbs dried oregano
1 tbs sweet paprika
3 garlic cloves, crushed
1/4 cup (60ml) extra virgin
    olive oil
2 tbs sunflower oil
1kg piece skinless salmon
    fillet, pin-boned

Papaya mojo

1/4 cup (60ml) extra virgin
    olive oil
1 small red onion, thinly sliced
1 papaya, cut into cubes
2 x 400g cans black turtle
    beans*, drained, rinsed
1 bunch coriander, leaves
    roughly chopped
Finely grated zest and juice
    of 2 limes, plus extra lime
    halves to serve

Preheat the oven to 180°C.

Place the oregano, paprika, garlic and olive oil in a bowl and season. Place the fish on a chopping board and rub the marinade into the topside of the fish.

Place the sunflower oil in a flameproof, non-stick roasting pan over high heat. Warm for 1-2 minutes until the oil is smoking, then add the fish, marinated-side down, and cook for 5-6 minutes until the flesh has blackened. Transfer to the oven, then bake for 10 minutes or until just cooked, but still a little rare in the centre.

Meanwhile, for the papaya mojo, place all the ingredients together in a bowl, season, then gently toss to combine. Set aside.

Invert the fish onto a platter and top with papaya mojo. Serve with the lime halves. **Serves 6-8**

* Available from delis and gourmet food shops.

SUMMER ROAST LAMB WITH ROCKET CREAM

1¹/2 cups (100g) fresh
  breadcrumbs
²/3 cup (50g) finely
  grated parmesan
¹/4 cup (40g) pine nuts, toasted
1¹/2 cups rocket,
  plus extra to serve
¹/2 cup basil leaves
³/4 cup (185ml) extra virgin
  olive oil
4 x 4- or 5-cutlet lamb racks
2 tbs wholegrain mustard
250g punnet vine-ripened
  cherry tomatoes
600g waxy potatoes (such as
  kipfler), boiled, halved
200g green beans, blanched
2 tbs lemon juice

Rocket cream
¹/2 cup (150g) whole-egg
  mayonnaise
100g creme fraiche
3 cups rocket
1 garlic clove, crushed
1 tbs wholegrain mustard

Preheat the oven to 190°C.

For the rocket cream, place all the ingredients in a food processor, season, then whiz until smooth. Keep chilled until ready to serve.

Place the breadcrumbs, parmesan, pine nuts, rocket and basil in a small food processor, season, then whiz to combine. With the motor running, slowly add 100ml oil until a coarse paste forms. Set aside.

Place 1 tablespoon oil in a large frypan over medium-high heat. Season the lamb, cook in batches, for 2-3 minutes each side until browned, then allow to cool completely. Brush the meat-side of each rack with the mustard, then pat on the pesto crumb mixture. Place the lamb racks on a baking tray, then roast for 5 minutes. Add the tomatoes to the tray and roast for a further 5 minutes for rare lamb or until cooked to your liking and the tomatoes have softened. Rest lamb, loosely covered with foil, for 5 minutes.

Place the tomatoes, potatoes, beans, lemon juice and remaining ¹/4 cup (60ml) oil in a bowl. Season, then toss to combine.

Arrange the lamb and vegetables on a platter and serve with extra rocket and the rocket cream.
Serves 4-6

STEAK FAJITAS WITH HARISSA MAYONNAISE

Skirt steak is a popular cut of beef in Latin American cuisine. It's a relatively inexpensive cut that's available from most butchers.

1kg piece skirt steak

1 bunch coriander

3 garlic cloves, finely chopped

3$1/2$ tbs harissa (North African chilli paste)*

100ml extra virgin olive oil

1$1/2$ cups (450g) whole-egg mayonnaise

4 cobs corn, cooked, kernels sliced

2 avocados, chopped

1 red onion, finely chopped

1 roasted red capsicum, chopped

Finely grated zest and juice of 2 limes

Flour tortillas, to serve

Lightly score the steak on both sides. Finely chop the coriander stalks, reserving the leaves, then place the stalks in a bowl with the garlic, 2 tablespoons harissa and $1/4$ cup (60ml) oil. Season, then rub all over the steak. Cover, then marinate in the fridge for 3-4 hours.

Meanwhile, place the mayonnaise and remaining 1$1/2$ tablespoons harissa in a bowl and stir to combine. Keep chilled until ready to serve.

Roughly chop the reserved coriander leaves and place in a separate bowl with the corn kernels, avocado, onion, capsicum, lime zest and juice and remaining 2 tablespoons olive oil. Season, then toss well to combine.

Preheat a barbecue or chargrill pan over medium-high heat. Cook the steak for 3-4 minutes each side until charred, but still rare in the centre. Rest in a warm spot for 10 minutes.

Meanwhile, enclose the tortillas in foil and warm on the barbecue or in the chargrill pan.

Spread some harissa mayonnaise on each tortilla. Slice the steak, then divide among the tortillas and serve with the corn salsa. **Serves 6**

* From Middle Eastern and gourmet food shops.

CHICKEN & PANCETTA PICNIC ROLL

1/2 cup (100g) instant couscous
1 tbs sundried tomato paste
3/4 cup (185ml) chicken stock,
   heated
50g unsalted butter
1 onion, finely chopped
1/3 cup (50g) pine nuts, toasted
2/3 cup (100g) chopped
   semi-dried tomatoes
2 tbs chopped flat-leaf
   parsley leaves
2 tbs chopped mint leaves
1 egg, lightly beaten
6 x 170g chicken breast fillets
20 long flat pancetta slices*
Mixed salad leaves, to serve

Place couscous in a bowl with the sundried tomato paste. Pour in the hot stock, stirring to combine, then cover and stand for 5 minutes or until all the liquid has been absorbed. Fluff up with a fork.

Melt 25g butter in a frypan over medium heat. Cook the onion, stirring, for 3-4 minutes until soft. Add the onion to the couscous with the pine nuts, tomato and herbs, then season and allow to cool. Stir the egg through the cooled couscous mixture.

Place each chicken breast between 2 sheets of baking paper and flatten with a meat mallet or heavy rolling pin to an even thickness of about 2cm.

Place a large piece of foil on a work surface and arrange the pancetta on top, slightly overlapping, so they form a sheet large enough to enclose the chicken. Lay the chicken on the pancetta to form a rectangle, making sure there are no gaps. Place the couscous mixture in a long line down the centre of the chicken.

Starting at 1 long end, roll up chicken and pancetta, using the foil to enclose tightly. Twist the ends of the foil to seal, then chill for at least 2-3 hours to firm up.

Preheat the oven to 180°C.

Place the foil-wrapped picnic roll on a baking tray and bake for 45 minutes. Melt remaining 25g butter, then unwrap the roll and brush with the melted butter. Bake, uncovered, for a further 25 minutes or until the pancetta is crisp and the chicken is cooked through. Cool for at least 1 hour, then cut into 2cm-thick slices. Serve with salad leaves. **Serves 8-10**

* Available from delis.

GREEN TEA YAKITORI WITH JAPANESE SEASONED RICE

Why have boring plain rice when you can pop into an Asian food shop and pick up a packet of furikake? This rice seasoning comes in a range of flavours, but here I've used Pandaroo sesame and seaweed blend.

1/3 cup (80ml) light soy sauce
2 tbs sweet chilli sauce
2 lemongrass stems (inner
 core only), grated
1 tsp chilli oil*
2 tsp loose-leaf green tea
1cm piece ginger, grated
2 tbs chopped coriander leaves
600g beef fillet steak,
 cut into 3cm pieces
1 1/2 cups (300g) jasmine rice
1/4 cup Japanese furikake
 seasoning*
Pickled ginger* and mizuna*,
 to serve

Place the soy sauce, sweet chilli sauce, lemongrass, chilli oil, green tea, ginger and coriander in a large bowl. Add beef, stirring to coat, then place in the fridge to marinate for at least 4 hours or overnight.

Place 12 small wooden skewers in a bowl of cold water and allow to soak for 1 hour.

Cook the rice according to the packet instructions.

Meanwhile, preheat a barbecue or chargrill pan over medium-high heat.

Drain the beef, then thread onto the soaked skewers. Cook the beef, turning, for 3-4 minutes for rare or until cooked to your liking.

Toss the rice with the furikake seasoning. Serve the beef skewers with seasoned rice, pickled ginger and mizuna. **Serves 4**

* From Asian food shops and selected supermarkets.

OCEAN TROUT MUFFULETTA

This Italian-style sandwich would have to be my favourite picnic fare. It's easy to transport and each delicious mouthful is full of surprises.

4 zucchinis, sliced lengthways

Olive oil, to brush

23cm pagnotta Italian loaf
  or cob loaf

²/3 cup (180g) pesto
  (see Extras, p 246)

6 hard-boiled eggs, sliced

100g rocket

Creme fraiche, to serve

Poached ocean trout

2 bay leaves

6 whole black peppercorns

1 onion, sliced

Pared zest of ¹/2 lemon

1kg piece skinless ocean trout
  fillet, pin-boned

Begin this recipe a day ahead.

For the poached ocean trout, place the bay leaves, peppercorns, onion and lemon zest in a flameproof roasting pan large enough to hold the fish. Add 4 litres water, then bring to the boil. Carefully slide the fish into the water, adding extra boiling water to ensure the fish is completely covered. Remove from the heat, then cover with foil and stand for 20 minutes or until the fish is just cooked, but still a little rare in the centre. Remove the fish from the poaching liquid and allow to cool. Flake into large pieces and set aside.

Preheat a barbecue or chargrill pan over medium-high heat.

Brush the zucchini with oil and grill for 1-2 minutes each side until tender and charred.

Slice the top off the bread and set aside, then hollow out the centre, leaving a 2cm-thick layer inside the crust. Brush the inside of the loaf with a little pesto.

Arrange half the trout in the base of the loaf, then top with half the zucchini. Spread with half the remaining pesto, then top with half the egg. Repeat the layers, then replace the bread top and enclose tightly in plastic wrap. Place in the fridge and top with a baking tray weighed down with cans. Chill overnight.

The next day, slice into wedges and serve with creme fraiche. **Serves 6**

PEPPERED TUNA WITH GREEN TEA NOODLES

4 x 180g tuna steaks
$^1/_3$ cup (80ml) sunflower oil
2 tbs sansho pepper*
  or Szechuan pepper*
200g green tea soba noodles*
1 cup frozen, podded
  edamame (soy beans)*
2 tbs mirin (Japanese
  rice wine)*
2 tbs soy sauce
1 tbs rice vinegar
1 tsp sesame oil
Seaweed salad (wakame)*,
  to serve

Brush the tuna steaks with 1 tablespoon sunflower oil. Mix sansho or Szechuan pepper, 2 tablespoons freshly ground black pepper and 1 teaspoon sea salt in a bowl, then rub onto the tuna. Set aside while you cook the noodles.

Cook the noodles in boiling, salted water according to the packet instructions, adding the edamame for the final 3 minutes of cooking time. Drain and refresh under cold water. Set aside.

Place 1 tablespoon sunflower oil on the flat plate of a barbecue or in a frypan over medium-high heat. Cook the tuna for 1 minute each side for rare.

Place the mirin, soy sauce, rice vinegar, sesame oil and remaining 2 tablespoons sunflower oil in a bowl, stirring to combine, then toss with the noodles and edamame. Divide the noodles among plates and top with the tuna. Serve with the seaweed salad. **Serves 4**

* Available from Asian food shops.

BUTTERMILK PUDDING WITH BERRIES AND CHERRIES

I make this pudding using a pyramid mould, available from kitchenware shops, but you can use any 1 litre terrine mould or loaf pan.

150ml milk

1/4 cup (55g) caster sugar

1 vanilla bean, split, seeds scraped

4 gold-strength gelatine leaves*

600ml buttermilk

125g punnet blueberries

125g punnet raspberries

250g punnet strawberries, halved if large

200g jar amarena cherries in syrup*

Almond bread, to serve

Begin this recipe a day ahead.

Place the milk, sugar and vanilla pod and seeds in a small saucepan over medium-low heat, stirring until the sugar dissolves. Bring to just below boiling point, then remove from the heat.

Soak the gelatine leaves in a bowl of cold water for 5 minutes. Squeeze excess water from the gelatine leaves, then add the leaves to the warm milk mixture, whisking gently until the gelatine dissolves. Stir in the buttermilk, then strain into a 1 litre pyramid mould. Allow to cool, then chill overnight.

The next day, place the berries and cherries with the syrup in a bowl. Stand for 10 minutes to macerate.

To unmould the pudding, dip the base of the mould briefly in hot water, then turn out onto a platter. Cut into slices, then serve with the berries and cherries and the almond bread. **Serves 6-8**

* Available from gourmet food shops.

MERINGUES WITH MANGO MOJITO SAUCE

This is my foolproof method for meringues. I find warming the eggwhites and sugar first ensures the sugar dissolves, resulting in a crisp meringue with a soft, mallowy centre. The unfilled meringues will keep in an airtight container for up to 2 days.

4 eggwhites
250g caster sugar
2 tsp cornflour
1 tsp white wine vinegar
2-3 drops yellow
   food colouring
300ml thickened cream,
   lightly whipped

Mango mojito sauce

2 large mangoes, chopped,
   plus extra mango to serve
1/4 cup (60ml) white rum
1 tbs lime juice
1 tbs chopped mint leaves,
   plus extra leaves to serve
1/3 cup (75g) caster sugar

Preheat the oven to 140°C and line a baking tray with baking paper.

Place the eggwhites and sugar in a heatproof bowl set over a saucepan of gently simmering water (don't let the bowl touch the water). Whisk constantly for 6-8 minutes until the sugar has dissolved and the mixture is thick. Transfer to an electric mixer and continue to whisk for 10 minutes or until the meringue mixture is cool, stiff and glossy. Fold in the cornflour and vinegar, then use a skewer to swirl the yellow food colouring through the meringue.

Place 6 dollops of meringue mixture on the baking tray, making a shallow indent in the centre of each with the back of a spoon. Bake for 1 hour, then turn off the oven and allow the meringues to cool completely in the oven with the door slightly ajar.

Meanwhile, for the mango mojito sauce, whiz all the ingredients together in a food processor until smooth.

Top the meringues with the whipped cream, then garnish with extra mango and mint leaves. Serve drizzled with the mango mojito sauce. **Serves 6**

STRAWBERRY TART WITH BASIL CREAM

Just for presentation, I like to keep some of the strawberries unhulled.
The bright green leaves add an extra burst of colour to this tart.

200g amaretti (Italian
  almond biscuits)*
125g unsalted butter,
  melted, cooled
2 x 250g punnets strawberries,
  halved if large
2 tbs icing sugar, sifted,
  plus extra to serve
600ml thickened cream
2 tsp finely grated lime zest
Pulp of 2 passionfruit
6 large basil leaves,
  finely chopped
1/3 cup (95g) thick
  Greek-style yoghurt

Grease a 22cm loose-bottomed tart pan.

Place the amaretti in a food processor and whiz to fine crumbs. Add the butter and pulse a few times to combine, then press into the base and sides of the tart pan. Chill for 30 minutes to firm up.

Place the strawberries in a bowl and toss with the icing sugar. Set aside.

Place the cream and lime zest in separate bowl and beat with electric beaters until stiff peaks form. Strain the passionfruit pulp into the cream mixture, pressing down with the back of a spoon to extract as much juice as possible and discarding the seeds, then gently fold to combine. Fold in the basil and yoghurt.

Fill the tart shell with the basil cream and arrange the strawberries on top. Serve the tart dusted with extra icing sugar. **Serves 6-8**

* Available from delis and gourmet food shops.

FROZEN CHOCOLATE ZUCCOTTO

Zuccotto is a chilled Italian dessert from Florence. It has an outer layer of sponge cake that's filled with ricotta or ice cream.

2 rectangular 30cm x 20cm
   chocolate sponge cakes
   (see Extras, p 246)
$1/2$ cup (125ml) amaretto
   liqueur
400g fresh ricotta,
   well drained
$1/2$ cup (75g) icing sugar
100g dark chocolate, finely
   chopped, plus extra melted
   dark chocolate to serve
$1/3$ cup (55g) blanched
   almonds, toasted, chopped
$1/3$ cup (85g) chopped
   glacé cherries
2 tbs chopped stem ginger
   in syrup*, drained
600ml thickened cream,
   lightly whipped

Begin this recipe a day ahead.

Using a 2 litre pudding basin as a template, cut a circle from 1 cake, reserving trimmings, and set aside.

Line the pudding basin with plastic wrap, leaving plenty overhanging the sides. Line the base and sides of the basin with the remaining cake, cutting to fit. Brush the cake with 2 tablespoons amaretto. Set aside.

Place the ricotta and icing sugar in a bowl and beat with electric beaters until smooth. Fold the chopped chocolate, almond, cherry, ginger and remaining $1/3$ cup (80ml) amaretto into the ricotta mixture until just combined, then fold in the whipped cream.

Spoon the ricotta mixture into the cake-lined basin, then smooth the surface with the back of the spoon. Top with the reserved cake circle, then cover with the overhanging plastic wrap. Freeze overnight.

The next day, invert the zuccotto onto a plate and cut into slices. Serve drizzled with melted chocolate. **Serves 6-8**

* Available from delis and selected supermarkets.

COCONUT & MANGO TARTS WITH CHILLI SYRUP

1 quantity coconut pastry
(see Extras, p 246) or 435g
packet Careme Vanilla Bean
Sweet Shortcrust Pastry*
100g unsalted butter
1/2 cup (125ml) coconut cream
250g white chocolate
2 tbs Malibu or other coconut
liqueur (optional)
2 mangoes, thinly sliced

Chilli syrup

2 long red chillies, seeds
removed, finely chopped
1/2 cup (110g) caster sugar
Juice of 1 lime

Preheat the oven to 180°C. Lightly grease six 10cm loose-bottomed tart pans.

Roll out the pastry to 5mm thick if using homemade. Use the pastry to line the tart pans, trimming the excess. Chill for 10 minutes.

Line the tart shells with baking paper and fill with pastry weights or uncooked rice, then bake for 10 minutes. Remove the paper and weights, then bake for a further 5 minutes or until golden and dry. Allow to cool completely in the pans.

Place the butter and coconut cream in a saucepan over medium-low heat, stirring until the butter melts. Remove from the heat, then add the chocolate, stirring until melted and smooth. Stir in the Malibu, if using, then pour the coconut cream mixture into the cooled tart shells. Chill for 2 hours or until set.

Meanwhile, for the chilli syrup, place all ingredients and 1 1/2 cups (375ml) water in a saucepan over low heat, stirring until the sugar dissolves. Simmer, stirring occasionally, for 20 minutes or until thickened and small bubbles appear on the surface. Remove from the heat and allow to cool completely.

Arrange the mango on top of the tarts, then serve drizzled with the chilli syrup. **Serves 6**

* From delis and gourmet food shops; for stockists, visit: caremepastry.com.

SUMMER PUDDING WITH ROSE-SCENTED CUSTARD

When making summer pudding, I ask my baker to slice a loaf of bread lengthways so it's easier to line the loaf pan, but you could use 15 or so slices of pre-cut bread instead.

1kg mixed fresh or frozen, thawed berries, plus extra to serve
1 cup (220g) caster sugar
2 tsp lemon juice
2 gold-strength gelatine leaves*
1 loaf day-old white bread, crusts removed, thinly sliced lengthways
Unsprayed fresh rose petals and icing sugar, to serve

Rose-scented custard

2 tsp rosewater*
1-2 drops pink food colouring
2½ cups (625ml) chilled custard (see Extras, p 246)

Place the berries and caster sugar in a saucepan over low heat, stirring until the sugar dissolves and the berries start to release their juices. Stir in the lemon juice and add a little more sugar to taste, if necessary. Strain into a bowl, reserving the berries. Reserve ¼ cup (60ml) berry juice and return the remaining juice to the saucepan. Cook over low heat for 2-3 minutes or until slightly reduced.

Soak the gelatine leaves in a bowl of cold water for 5 minutes. Squeeze out excess water, then add the gelatine leaves to the warm syrup, stirring to dissolve.

Line a 1 litre loaf pan with plastic wrap, leaving plenty overhanging the sides, then place on a baking tray. Line the base and sides of the pan with half the bread slices. Fill with half the reserved berries and top with a layer of bread. Drizzle with half the berry syrup, then repeat the layers. Cover tightly with plastic wrap, then top with a piece of cardboard cut to fit and weigh down with cans. Chill for at least 4 hours or overnight.

The next day, for the rose-scented custard, stir the rosewater and food colouring into the chilled custard.

Invert pudding onto a plate and brush any exposed white bread with the reserved ¼ cup (60ml) berry juice. Slice the pudding and garnish with rose petals and extra berries, then dust with icing sugar. Serve with the rose-scented custard. **Serves 6-8**

* Available from gourmet food shops.

TROPICAL FRUIT SALAD WITH GREEN TEA ICE CREAM

^{1}/$_2$ cup (110g) caster sugar

1 lemongrass stem (inner core only), bruised

1 star anise

3cm piece ginger, peeled, bruised

1 kiwi fruit, sliced

1 dragon fruit, sliced

1 star fruit, sliced

1 mango, sliced

1 papaya, sliced

Unsprayed edible flowers* (optional), to serve

Green tea ice cream

1 cup (250ml) milk

2 egg yolks

2 tbs caster sugar

2 tbs green tea powder (matcha)*, mixed with ^{1}/$_4$ cup (60ml) boiling water

2-3 drops green food colouring

300ml thickened cream, lightly whipped

For the ice cream, place the milk in a saucepan over medium heat and bring to just below boiling point. Remove from heat. Place the egg yolks and sugar in a bowl and beat with electric beaters until thick and pale. Pour the hot milk into the yolk mixture, stirring constantly, then pour into a clean saucepan over low heat. Cook, stirring constantly, for 4-5 minutes until thick enough to coat the back of a spoon. Cool slightly. Stir the green tea mixture and food colouring into the custard, then transfer to a bowl and cover the surface closely with a piece of baking paper. Chill for 30 minutes or until cold. Fold the whipped cream through the cooled custard, then churn in an ice cream machine according to the manufacturer's instructions. (Alternatively, pour into a shallow container and freeze for 2 hours or until frozen at the edges. Remove from the freezer and beat with electric beaters. Repeat the process 2-3 times.) Freeze for 4 hours or until firm.

Meanwhile, place the sugar, spices and 2^1/$_2$ cups (625ml) water in a saucepan over low heat, stirring until sugar dissolves. Simmer for 2 minutes, then cool.

Place the sliced fruits in a bowl and pour over the spiced sugar syrup. Stand for 30 minutes to macerate.

Garnish the fruit salad with edible flowers, if desired, and serve with the green tea ice cream. **Serves 4-6**

* Edible flowers are available from farmers' markets and selected greengrocers. Green tea powder (matcha) is available from Asian food shops.

FIRE & ICE CAKE

This is one show-stopping dessert. Once you've mastered the toffee shard assembly, all you have to do is wait for the applause.

250g shortbread biscuits
100g unsalted butter, melted, cooled
6 egg yolks
1/4 cup (60ml) Marsala (Sicilian fortified wine)
1/2 cup (110g) caster sugar
900ml thickened cream, lightly whipped
1 1/2 tsp vanilla extract
250g white sugar
1/2 cup (125ml) golden syrup
2-3 drops red food colouring
Strawberries and raspberries, to serve

Begin this recipe a day ahead.

Place the biscuits in a food processor and whiz to fine crumbs. Add the butter and pulse a few times to combine, then press into the base of a greased 22cm springform cake pan. Chill while you make the filling.

Place the egg yolks, Marsala and caster sugar in a heatproof bowl set over a saucepan of gently simmering water (don't let the bowl touch the water). Whisk constantly for 3-4 minutes until thick and pale. Remove from heat, then place the bowl in a larger bowl of iced water (don't let any water splash into the yolk mixture), whisking occasionally until cooled and voluminous. Fold the whipped cream and 1 teaspoon vanilla into the cooled yolk mixture. Pour over the biscuit base and freeze overnight.

The next day, line 2 baking trays with baking paper. Place the white sugar, golden syrup and 1/2 cup (125ml) water in a saucepan over low heat, stirring until sugar dissolves. Cook, swirling the pan occasionally, for 4-5 minutes until a golden caramel. Add the red food colouring and the remaining 1/2 teaspoon vanilla and swirl to combine. Dip a fork into the caramel, then drizzle the caramel onto the baking trays to create long strands. Set aside for 15 minutes to harden.

Remove cake from the freezer. Break the caramel into long wide shards and press onto the sides of the cake. Top the cake with the berries and serve immediately. **Serves 8-10**

SIMPLE APRICOT TART

For this tart, I use marzipan to make a cheat's frangipane. Then it's only a matter of assembling everything together and placing in the oven for a simple summer dessert.

375g block frozen puff pastry, thawed
120g marzipan
2 tbs thickened cream, plus extra to serve
8 apricots, halved
2 tbs honey
Icing sugar and chopped pistachios, to serve

Preheat the oven to 200°C and line a baking tray with baking paper.

Roll out the pastry to a 20cm x 30cm rectangle and place on the baking tray. Chill for 10 minutes.

Place the marzipan and cream in a food processor and whiz until smooth. Spread over the pastry base, leaving a 2cm border. Place the apricots, cut-side up, on the marzipan mixture, then drizzle with the honey. Bake for 25 minutes or until the pastry is puffed and golden and the apricots are starting to caramelise.

Dust the tart with icing sugar and scatter with pistachios. Serve with extra cream. **Serves 4-6**

SUMMER MENUS

Sunday lunch

STARTER
Ginger & chilli
kingfish ceviche

MAIN
Summer roast lamb
with rocket cream

DESSERT
Buttermilk pudding with
berries and cherries

20

36

48

22

40

52

Al fresco feast

STARTER
Potted trout with
dill cucumbers

MAIN
Chicken & pancetta
picnic roll

DESSERT
Strawberry tart
with basil cream

seafood dinner party

STARTER
Little seafood tarts

MAIN
Blackened salmon
with papaya mojo

DESSERT
Fire & ice cake

24

34

62

18

28

64

Lazy day brunch

STARTER
Tomato, goat's cheese
& poppyseed tartines

MAIN
Mexican corn cakes with
avocado and prawns

DESSERT
Simple apricot tart

AUTUMN

in season

pomegranates
apples avocados beans (borlotti, butter, green)
celery chestnuts fennel figs grapes kumara
leeks nashi olives oranges parsnips pears
plums pumpkins quince sugar snap peas

BLUE CHEESE CUSTARDS WITH A LITTLE AUTUMN SALAD

These simple little custards are savoury versions of that classic Italian dessert, panna cotta. If you like, replace the sharp gorgonzola picante with a milder goat's cheese instead.

4 gold-strength gelatine
   leaves*
200ml milk
300ml pure (thin) cream
150g gorgonzola picante or
   other strong blue cheese
Vincotto*, chopped pistachios
   and toasted baguette slices,
   to serve

Little autumn salad

1 green apple,
   cut into matchsticks
2 tsp lemon juice
2 cups mixed micro herbs
   or flat-leaf parsley leaves
2 tbs extra virgin olive oil

Soak the gelatine leaves in a bowl of cold water for 5 minutes.

Meanwhile, place milk and cream in a saucepan over medium heat and bring to just below boiling point. Remove from the heat, then crumble the gorgonzola into the warm milk mixture and whisk briefly until combined. Season.

Squeeze excess water from the gelatine leaves, then add the leaves to the warm milk mixture, whisking gently until the gelatine dissolves. Strain into a jug, then pour into 4 lightly greased $1/2$ cup (125ml) ramekins. Chill for at least 4 hours or overnight to set.

For the salad, toss the apple with the lemon juice, then place in a bowl with the herbs. Drizzle with olive oil, season, then toss to combine.

To unmould the custards, dip the base of the ramekins briefly in hot water, then turn out onto plates. Drizzle with the vincotto, top with pistachios and serve with the toasted baguette and salad.
Serves 4

* Gelatine leaves and vincotto (a condiment made from cooked grape must) are available from gourmet food shops.

CELERIAC & PARMESAN SOUP WITH ORANGE GREMOLATA

This velvety soup is just the thing to warm you up on a cool night. For added depth of flavour, add the parmesan rind to the soup, then remove and discard before blending.

60g unsalted butter
1 large celeriac (about 1.2kg), peeled, chopped
1 onion, chopped
1$\frac{1}{4}$ cups (100g) finely grated parmesan
1L (4 cups) chicken stock
300ml thickened cream
1 tbs truffle oil* or extra virgin olive oil, plus extra to drizzle
Grilled sourdough, to serve

Orange gremolata

$\frac{1}{4}$ cup finely chopped flat-leaf parsley
2 garlic cloves, finely chopped
Finely grated zest of 1 orange
1 tbs grated parmesan
1 tbs extra virgin olive oil

Melt the butter in a saucepan over low heat. Add the celeriac and onion, season, then cover with a lid and cook, stirring occasionally, for 20 minutes or until tender. Add the parmesan and stock and bring to a simmer over medium-low heat. Cook for 5 minutes, then stir in the cream and oil. Reduce heat to low and cook for a further 5 minutes. Remove the soup from the heat, then use a stick blender to puree until smooth. (Alternatively, cool slightly, then puree in batches in a blender.) Pass the soup through a fine sieve into a clean saucepan.

Meanwhile, for the gremolata, combine all the ingredients in a small bowl. Set aside.

Reheat the soup over low heat, then ladle into serving bowls. Scatter with the gremolata and drizzle with oil. Serve with grilled bread. **Serves 6-8**

* Available from delis and gourmet food shops.

BEEF TATAKI

300g piece centre-cut
    beef eye fillet, trimmed
2 tbs olive oil
2 tbs shichimi togarashi
    (Japanese spice mix)*
4 radishes, cut into
    matchsticks
1/4 daikon (white radish),
    cut into matchsticks
1 small carrot, cut into
    matchsticks
Micro coriander or regular
    coriander leaves, to serve

Dressing
2 tbs soy sauce
1 tbs rice vinegar
1 tbs lime juice
1/2 tsp wasabi paste,
    plus extra to serve
1 garlic clove, crushed
1 tsp grated ginger
1 tsp caster sugar
1/2 tsp sesame oil

Brush the beef with 1 tablespoon oil, season, then coat in the shichimi togarashi. Place the remaining 1 tablespoon oil in a frypan over high heat. Cook the beef, turning, for 2-3 minutes until browned on all sides. Cool, then enclose the beef in plastic wrap and freeze for 1 hour (this will make it easier to slice).

Meanwhile, for the dressing, whisk all the ingredients together in a small bowl. Set aside.

Unwrap beef, then slice the beef wafer thin and place on a platter or individual serving plates. Scatter with the radish, daikon and carrot, then drizzle over the dressing. Garnish with coriander and serve with extra wasabi. **Serves 6**

* Available from Asian food shops and selected supermarkets.

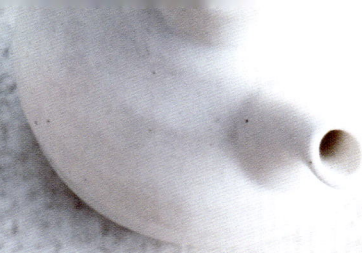

ANTIPASTO PLATTER WITH ARTICHOKE DIP

A simple antipasto platter is an easy starter for a casual dinner. Just pick up some salami, olives and Italian cheese from your local deli, then bring it all together with a homemade dip. You could also add some chargrilled vegetables or bocconcini – it's really up to you.

280g jar marinated artichokes, drained
400g can butter beans, rinsed, drained
1 garlic clove, chopped
1/2 cup flat-leaf parsley leaves
2 tbs extra virgin olive oil
1 tsp ground cumin
1 tsp sweet paprika
Juice of 1/2 lemon
Marinated olives, salami, breadsticks, crispbread and a wedge of Italian cheese (such as gorgonzola dolce), to serve

Place the artichokes, beans, garlic, parsley, olive oil, spices and lemon juice in a food processor, season, then whiz to combine. With the motor running, add 2-3 tablespoons warm water to form a smooth paste.

Place the artichoke dip in a serving dish and set it on a large platter with the olives, salami, breadsticks, crispbread and a wedge of Italian cheese. **Serves 4**

FIG, LABNE & BRESAOLA SALAD

This is another easy dish using some of my favourite ingredients from the deli. I simply jazz up labne with dukkah and lemony spice sumac, then pair it with some bresaola.

1/2 cup (60g) dukkah
1 tsp sumac
370g jar marinated labne
   (yoghurt cheese)
1/4 cup (60ml) lemon juice
1 frisée (curly endive), outer
   leaves removed
1 cup mint leaves
1 cup flat-leaf parsley leaves
1/2 red onion, thinly sliced
6 figs, quartered
18 thin slices bresaola
   (cured, air-dried beef)
Grilled Turkish bread, to serve

Combine dukkah and sumac in a bowl. Drain the labne, reserving the oil, then roll the labne balls in the dukkah mixture. Chill for 30 minutes.

Whisk lemon juice and 1/3 cup (80ml) reserved oil together in a small bowl. Season and set aside.

Roughly chop frisée and place in a bowl with the herbs and onion, then toss to combine. Pile the salad onto serving plates and arrange the figs and bresaola on top. Scatter over the dukkah-crusted labne, drizzle with the dressing and serve with grilled Turkish bread.

Serves 6

BEETROOT RISOTTO WITH MELTING BRIE

350g beetroot, peeled,
  cut into 1cm cubes
1L (4 cups) chicken or
  vegetable stock
1 tbs olive oil
1 onion, finely chopped
3 garlic cloves, chopped
250g arborio rice
100ml white wine
50g unsalted butter
A few thyme sprigs,
  leaves picked
1¼ cups (100g) finely
  grated parmesan,
  plus extra to serve
120g buche d'Affinois or
  other ripe double-cream
  brie, thickly sliced
Mixed micro herbs or extra
  thyme leaves, to serve

Place the beetroot and stock in a saucepan, bring to a simmer over medium heat and cook for 10-15 minutes until beetroot is tender. Drain the beetroot, reserving the stock. Set beetroot aside. Return stock to the pan and place over low heat.

Meanwhile, heat the oil in a separate saucepan over medium-low heat. Add onion and cook, stirring, for 1-2 minutes until softened. Add the garlic and rice, stirring for 1-2 minutes to coat the grains, then add the wine and allow to bubble until almost evaporated.

Stir in the stock, a ladleful at a time, allowing each to be absorbed before adding the next. Continue to cook, stirring constantly, until all the stock has been absorbed and rice is al dente – this should take about 20 minutes. Stir in the reserved beetroot.

Remove the pan from the heat. Stir in the butter, thyme leaves and parmesan, then season. Stand for 2 minutes, then divide risotto among shallow bowls. Sprinkle with extra parmesan and top with a slice of brie, allowing it to melt slightly. Sprinkle with herbs and serve. **Serves 4-6**

MEXICAN CHICKEN & RICE SOUP

This zesty, spicy soup warms the soul and makes the most of my new-found love of Mexican flavours. It makes a great light lunch or supper, too.

2 garlic cloves, finely chopped
2L (8 cups) chicken stock
1/2 cup (100g) long-grain rice
1 small red onion, thinly sliced
1 jalapeno chilli, seeds
  removed, finely chopped
2 cups (320g) shredded
  cooked chicken
2 tomatoes, seeds removed,
  chopped
2 tbs chopped coriander,
  plus extra leaves to serve
Juice of 1 lime, plus lime
  wedges to serve
2 spring onions, shredded
1 avocado, chopped
Toasted corn tortillas, to serve

Place the garlic and stock in a large saucepan and bring to a simmer over medium heat. Add the rice and cook for 10 minutes. Add onion and chilli, then simmer for a further 10 minutes or until the rice is tender. Add the chicken, tomato and coriander, then cook for a further 1 minute to warm through. Season, then add the lime juice to taste.

Ladle the soup into bowls, then top with spring onion and avocado. Serve with lime wedges and toasted corn tortillas. **Serves 4**

SCALLOPS WITH PUMPKIN AND SAGE BURNT BUTTER

400g pumpkin (such as Jap
   or butternut), peeled, cut
   into 2cm pieces
$1/4$ cup (60ml) chicken
   or vegetable stock
$1/4$ tsp ground nutmeg
40g unsalted butter
16 sage leaves
20 large scallops, roe removed
2 tbs toasted pine nuts

Preheat the oven to 180°C. Grease and line a baking tray with baking paper.

Place pumpkin on the baking tray and season. Cover with foil and roast for 40 minutes or until tender. Cool slightly, then place in a food processor with the stock and nutmeg. Whiz until smooth, then transfer to a saucepan and season. Cover and keep warm over low heat.

Meanwhile, melt the butter in a frypan over medium-high heat. When it starts to sizzle, add the sage leaves and cook for 1 minute or until crisp. Remove sage from the pan with a slotted spoon and drain on paper towel.

Remove 1 tablespoon butter from the pan and set aside. Season the scallops, then pan-fry, in batches, for 30 seconds each side or until just cooked, but still translucent in the centre. Remove the scallops from the pan, then return the reserved butter to the pan and cook for a further 1-2 minutes until the butter is nut brown.

To serve, divide pumpkin puree among serving plates, top with scallops and drizzle with the burnt butter. Scatter with crispy sage leaves and pine nuts, then serve. **Serves 4**

'FIGGY PIGGY'

Ripe figs and sweet prosciutto are a match made in heaven. Add a little soft Italian blue cheese and you have a dish that is nothing short of sublime.

12 ciabatta slices
Olive oil, to brush
1 garlic clove, halved
12 figs, torn in half
120g gorgonzola dolce or
    other mild blue cheese,
    crumbled
12 slices prosciutto
Mixed micro herbs or small
    basil leaves and vincotto* or
    balsamic vinegar, to serve

Heat a chargrill pan over high heat. Brush the bread with a little olive oil and grill for 1-2 minutes each side until charred. Rub the hot bread with the cut side of the garlic clove. Keep warm.

Meanwhile, brush the figs with a little olive oil and grill, torn-side down, for 1 minute or until lightly caramelised.

Scatter most of the cheese over the bread, drape with the prosciutto and top with figs. Top with herbs and remaining cheese, drizzle with vincotto and serve.
Serves 6

* Vincotto (a condiment made from cooked grape must) is available from gourmet food shops.

STIR-FRIED PRAWNS WITH ASIAN GREENS

3 bunches Asian greens (such
   as choy sum and bok choy),
   roughly chopped
1/4 cup (60ml) sunflower oil
300g peeled (tails intact)
   green prawns, deveined
2 garlic cloves, chopped
1 tbs ginger, grated
2 tsp sambal oelek
   (Indonesian chilli paste)*
1/4 cup (60ml) kecap manis
   (Indonesian sweet
   soy sauce)*
2 tbs oyster sauce
1/4 cup (60ml) chicken stock
   or water
Fried Asian shallots*, sliced
   red chilli, coriander leaves
   and steamed rice, to serve

Blanch the Asian greens in boiling, salted water for 30 seconds or until wilted. Drain and refresh.

Heat the oil in a wok over high heat. Add the prawns, garlic and ginger, then stir-fry for 1-2 minutes until fragrant and prawns are almost cooked through. Add the sambal oelek, kecap manis, oyster sauce and drained Asian greens, tossing to combine, then add stock. Cook for a further 1 minute to warm through, then divide among bowls, scatter with shallots, chilli and coriander. Serve immediately with rice. **Serves 4**

* From Asian food shops and selected supermarkets.

CHICKEN & TALEGGIO JALOUSIE

50g unsalted butter

1 tbs olive oil

1 leek (white part only),
  thinly sliced

250g Swiss brown
  mushrooms, sliced

2 tsp chopped thyme leaves

2 tsp plain flour

$1/2$ cup (125ml) chicken stock

$1/2$ cup (125ml) thickened
  cream

$2^1/2$ cups (400g) shredded
  cooked chicken

375g block frozen puff pastry,
  thawed

150g Taleggio or other
  washed rind cheese,
  rind removed, chopped

1 egg, lightly beaten

Place the butter and oil in a frypan over medium-low heat. Add the leek and cook, stirring, for 5 minutes or until softened. Add the mushroom and thyme, then cook, stirring, for 1-2 minutes until softened. Add the flour and cook, stirring, for 1 minute, then stir in the stock and cream. Cook for 1-2 minutes until the sauce is slightly thickened, then stir in the chicken and season well. Set aside to cool.

Preheat the oven to 200°C and line a baking tray with baking paper.

Roll out the pastry on a lightly floured surface to a 20cm x 40cm rectangle, then cut in half lengthways. Place 1 pastry half on the baking tray, then spread over chicken filling, leaving a 1cm border. Scatter with Taleggio and brush the pastry edges with egg.

Gently fold the remaining pastry in half lengthways. Use a sharp knife to make cuts at 1cm intervals down the folded side, leaving a 1cm border on the other side. Carefully open up the folded pastry and place over the filling, pressing the edges to seal – the pastry should separate slightly to reveal some of the filling. Brush all over with beaten egg and bake for 25 minutes or until puffed and golden. Cut into slices and serve. **Serves 4-6**

MEATBALLS WITH HEAVENLY MASH

250g pork mince
250g veal mince
250g lamb mince
4 garlic cloves,
    finely chopped
2 tbs fresh breadcrumbs
1 egg, lightly beaten
$1/2$ cup (120g) fresh ricotta
$1/4$ cup (20g) grated parmesan
$1/4$ cup chopped flat-leaf
    parsley, plus extra to serve
$1/4$ cup finely chopped basil
$1/4$ cup (60ml) olive oil
1 onion, finely chopped
1 anchovy fillet in oil, drained
750ml bottle tomato passata
    (sugo)
400g can chopped tomatoes
2 tsp caster sugar

Heavenly mash
1kg potatoes, peeled,
    chopped
$1/2$ cup (125ml) milk
$1/2$ cup (125ml) pure
    (thin) cream
1 cup (100g) grated fontina
    or other melting cheese
Unsalted butter, to serve

Place the mince, garlic, breadcrumbs, egg, ricotta, parmesan, parsley and basil in a bowl. Season well and use your hands to bring the mixture together. Shape into walnut-sized balls and chill for 30 minutes.

Heat 1 tablespoon olive oil in a large, deep frypan over medium-high heat. In batches, cook meatballs, turning, for 3-4 minutes until browned. Set aside.

Heat the remaining 2 tablespoons oil in the frypan over medium heat. Cook onion, stirring, for 2-3 minutes until softened. Add the anchovy, passata, chopped tomatoes and sugar, bring to a simmer, then reduce heat to low and cook for 5-6 minutes until slightly reduced. Add the meatballs and simmer for a further 5-6 minutes until the sauce is thick and the meatballs are cooked through.

Meanwhile, for the mash, cook the potatoes in boiling, salted water for 10-12 minutes until tender. Drain, then mash until smooth. Place the milk and cream in a small saucepan over medium-high heat and bring to just below boiling point. Beat milk mixture into the potatoes with a wooden spoon until smooth. Stir through the fontina, season, then top with a knob of butter.

Sprinkle the meatballs with extra parsley and serve with the heavenly mash. **Serves 4-6**

SCANDI SALMON

Salmon and beetroot has long been a favourite combination among my Scandinavian friends. It's the perfect way to bring together the best flavours of the earth and sea.

500g waxy potatoes (such as kipfler), thinly sliced

1 red onion, cut into wedges

1 bunch radishes, trimmed

1½ bunches baby beetroot, trimmed

2 tbs olive oil

4 x 180g skinless salmon fillets, pin-boned

1 tbs capers

2 tbs chopped dill

Beetroot yoghurt

¾ cup (200g) thick Greek-style yoghurt

1 tbs chopped dill

½ bunch baby beetroot, grated

Preheat the oven to 200°C.

Toss the potato, onion, radishes and beetroot with 1 tablespoon olive oil and season. Spread in a single layer on a baking tray and roast for 30 minutes or until potato and beetroot are tender.

Remove from the oven and turn the vegetables. Place the salmon fillets on top, season and drizzle with the remaining 1 tablespoon oil. Return to the oven for 6-8 minutes until the salmon is just cooked, but still a little rare in the centre.

Meanwhile, for the beetroot yoghurt, place yoghurt in a bowl and gently swirl through the dill and grated beetroot. Season and set aside.

Divide the vegetables and salmon fillets among plates. Top with capers and dill, then serve with the beetroot yoghurt. **Serves 4**

ZAATAR-CRUSTED LAMB WITH CHICKPEA & BEAN SALAD

4 x 150g lamb backstraps
1/4 cup (60ml) olive oil
1/4 cup (30g) zaatar (Middle
  Eastern spice blend)*
300g green beans, trimmed
400g can chickpeas, rinsed,
  drained
1 cup mint leaves, torn

Tahini dressing
1/2 cup (140g) tahini*
3 garlic cloves, crushed
Juice of 1 lemon
Pinch of cayenne pepper
Pinch of ground coriander
Pinch of ground cardamom

Rub the lamb with 2 tablespoons olive oil, then coat in the zaatar. Season, then set aside while you prepare the dressing and salad.

For the dressing, place all the ingredients in a blender and whiz to combine. With the motor running, slowly add 1/2 cup (125ml) warm water until you have a smooth dressing. Season and set aside.

Blanch the beans in boiling salted water for 2 minutes or until just tender. Drain, then refresh in iced water. Place the refreshed beans in a bowl with the chickpeas and mint.

Heat remaining 1 tablespoon oil in a frypan over medium-high heat and cook the lamb for 3 minutes each side for medium-rare or until cooked to your liking. Rest, loosely covered with foil, for 5 minutes.

Lightly toss half the tahini dressing with the salad. Thickly slice the lamb, then serve with the salad and remaining tahini dressing. **Serves 4**

* Available from delis and Middle Eastern food shops.

EGGPLANT & CHICKPEA CURRY

1 large eggplant (about 500g)
1 tbs sunflower oil
1 onion, chopped
2 tbs medium curry powder
400g can chopped tomatoes
400g can chickpeas, rinsed,
 drained
150g baby spinach
2 tbs mango chutney,
 plus extra to serve
Steamed basmati rice and
 pappadams, to serve

Preheat the oven to 200°C.

Prick the eggplant all over with a fork and place on a baking tray. Roast for 30 minutes or until tender and starting to collapse. Cool slightly.

Meanwhile, place the oil in a deep frypan (with a lid) over medium heat. Add the onion and cook, stirring, for 2-3 minutes until softened. Add the curry powder and cook, stirring, for 1 minute. Stir in the tomato, chickpeas and 200ml water, then reduce heat to low, cover and simmer for 10 minutes or until fragrant.

Chop the eggplant and stir into the curry with the spinach and mango chutney. Cook, uncovered, for 2-3 minutes until the spinach has wilted. Season, then serve with basmati rice, pappadams and extra mango chutney. **Serves 4**

MAKE-AHEAD LASAGNE

Lasagne is the perfect dish for entertaining because you can prepare it ahead and keep it in the fridge, then just bring it to room temperature and pop in the oven before your guests arrive. For a twist on tradition, I've replaced the bechamel sauce with ricotta.

1 tbs olive oil
500g beef mince
500g fresh ricotta
2 eggs, lightly beaten
1 cup basil leaves, chopped
1 1/2 cups (120g) finely
   grated parmesan
375g fresh lasagne sheets
600ml good-quality
   tomato pasta sauce
250g grated mozzarella
250g bocconcini, thinly sliced

Preheat the oven to 180°C. Grease a 22cm x 33cm baking dish.

Place the oil in a non-stick frypan over medium heat. Add the beef and cook, breaking up any lumps with a wooden spoon, for 6-8 minutes until browned. Set aside.

Combine the ricotta, egg, basil and half the parmesan in a bowl and season. Set aside.

Line the prepared baking dish with one-third of the lasagne sheets. Spread with one-third of the pasta sauce, then top with half the ricotta mixture and half the meat. Sprinkle with half the grated mozzarella. Repeat the layers, then top with the remaining pasta sheets and spread with the remaining pasta sauce. Arrange the sliced bocconcini on top, then sprinkle with the remaining parmesan. Cover with a layer of baking paper and a layer of foil. (If you like, you can pop the lasagne in the fridge at this stage and keep for up to 1 day.)

Bake lasagne for 30 minutes, then remove the foil and baking paper and bake for a further 20 minutes or until the lasagne is bubbling and golden. Stand for 15 minutes, then cut into slices and serve. **Serves 6-8**

MOROCCAN SWORDFISH WITH CHERMOULA AND POTATO SMASH

1kg waxy potatoes
   (such as kipfler)
4 x 180g swordfish steaks
100g rocket, roughly chopped
Micro herbs or coriander
   leaves, to serve

Chermoula
1 bunch coriander, chopped
2 small red chillies, seeds
   removed, finely chopped
4 garlic cloves, chopped
1 tsp ground cumin
1 tsp sweet paprika
1 tsp ground coriander
1/2 cup (125ml) extra virgin
   olive oil
Finely grated zest and juice
   of 2 lemons

For the chermoula, place all the ingredients in a blender. Season, then whiz to combine. Set aside.

Place the potatoes in a saucepan of cold, salted water. Bring to the boil over medium heat and cook for 15-20 minutes until tender. Drain, then return potatoes to the pan and roughly crush with a fork. Stir in two-thirds of the chermoula and keep warm.

Meanwhile, heat a chargrill pan or non-stick frypan over medium-high heat. Coat the swordfish in the remaining chermoula and cook for 2 minutes each side or until just cooked through.

To serve, fold the rocket into the potato smash and divide among plates. Place the swordfish on top and garnish with herbs. **Serves 4**

STICKY PORK CUTLETS WITH SPICY ASIAN SLAW

4 x 170g pork cutlets
1 tbs sunflower oil
2 tbs soy sauce
1 tbs honey

Spicy Asian slaw
$1/4$ white cabbage,
    finely shredded
$1/4$ red cabbage,
    finely shredded
1 carrot, finely shredded
1 red onion, thinly sliced
1 cup mint leaves
1 cup coriander leaves
1 kaffir lime leaf*,
    finely shredded
$1/4$ cup (60ml) rice vinegar
1 tbs caster sugar
2 tbs soy sauce
$1^{1}/2$ tbs lime juice
2 tbs fish sauce
2 long red chillies, seeds
    removed, finely chopped

For the Asian slaw, place the cabbage, carrot, onion, mint, coriander and kaffir lime leaf in a bowl. Combine rice vinegar, sugar, soy sauce, lime juice, fish sauce and chilli in a small bowl and whisk to combine. Toss the slaw with the dressing and set aside.

Drizzle the pork with the oil and season. Place a frypan over medium-high heat, then cook the pork for 2-3 minutes each side until golden. Reduce the heat to medium-low, then whisk the soy sauce and honey together and drizzle over the pork. Cook, turning, for a further 3-4 minutes until the pork chops are caramelised and cooked through.

Serve the pork with the spicy Asian slaw. **Serves 4**

* Available from greengrocers and Asian food shops.

CROISSANT & MARMALADE PUDDING

6 egg yolks

1/2 cup (110g) caster sugar

600ml pure (thin) cream,
  plus extra to serve

2 tsp vanilla extract

6 croissants (preferably
  day-old), split

40g unsalted butter, softened

3/4 cup (255g) fine-cut orange
  marmalade

Icing sugar, to serve

Grease a 1.2 litre baking dish.

Whisk the egg yolks, sugar, cream and vanilla together in a jug to combine. Set aside.

Spread the cut-side of the croissants with the butter and marmalade. Cut into large chunks and lightly pack into the prepared baking dish. Pour over the cream mixture and stand for 1 hour to allow the custard to soak in – this will result in a lighter pudding.

Preheat the oven to 160°C.

Place the baking dish in a deep roasting pan and pour enough boiling water into the roasting pan to come halfway up the sides of the dish. Bake the pudding for 1 hour or until golden and the custard is set. Stand for 15 minutes.

Dust the marmalade croissant pudding with icing sugar and serve warm with cream. **Serves 6-8**

CLASSIC CHOCOLATE CAKE

Every cook needs a knock-out chocolate cake recipe. This one is dense, rich and always a crowd pleaser. A simple chocolate icing is all you need for a spectacular finish.

200g dark chocolate, chopped
$1^{1}/_{3}$ cups (200g) plain flour
2 tbs cocoa powder
1 tsp baking powder
$^{1}/_{2}$ tsp bicarbonate of soda
225g unsalted butter,
    softened
1 cup (220g) caster sugar
4 eggs
1 tsp vanilla extract
$^{1}/_{2}$ cup (125ml) milk

Rich chocolate icing
250g dark chocolate, chopped
400g unsalted butter,
    softened
$2^{1}/_{3}$ cups (350g) icing sugar,
    sifted

Preheat the oven to 160°C. Grease and line a 23cm springform cake pan with baking paper.

Place the chocolate in a heatproof bowl set over a saucepan of gently simmering water (don't let the bowl touch the water), stirring until melted and smooth. Set aside to cool.

Sift flour, cocoa, baking powder, bicarbonate of soda and a pinch of salt into a bowl. Set aside.

Place the butter and caster sugar in a separate bowl and beat with electric beaters until thick and pale. Add the eggs, 1 at a time, beating well after each addition. Add cooled chocolate and vanilla and beat well to combine. Fold in the flour mixture, then add the milk and gently stir to combine.

Spread the batter into the cake pan and bake for 45-50 minutes until a skewer inserted into the centre comes out clean. Cool in the pan for 15 minutes, then transfer to a wire rack to cool completely.

For the icing, place the chocolate in a heatproof bowl set over a saucepan of gently simmering water (don't let the bowl touch the water), stirring until melted and smooth, then cool. Place butter and sifted icing sugar in a separate bowl and beat with electric beaters for 6-8 minutes until very thick and pale. Carefully fold in the cooled chocolate. Spread the icing over the cooled cake and serve. **Serves 8-10**

CHAI PANNA COTTA WITH POACHED QUINCES

600ml milk

1 cinnamon quill

6 cloves

6 cardamom pods

1 tsp fennel seeds

1 tsp mixed spice

1 tbs English breakfast
    tea leaves

1/2 cup (110g) caster sugar

1 vanilla bean, split,
    seeds scraped

6 gold-strength gelatine
    leaves*

600ml thickened cream,
    whipped to soft peaks

Ground cinnamon, to serve

Poached quinces

6 small quinces, peeled,
    cut into wedges

2 cups (440g) caster sugar

2 cinnamon quills

6 cloves

Thinly pared rind of 1 lemon

1 vanilla bean, split,
    seeds scraped

Place the milk, spices, tea, sugar and vanilla pod and seeds in a saucepan over medium heat, stirring until sugar dissolves. Bring to just below boiling point, then reduce heat to low and cook for 5 minutes. Remove from the heat and stand for 5 minutes to infuse.

Meanwhile, soak the gelatine leaves in cold water for 5 minutes to soften. Squeeze out excess water, then add the gelatine to the warm milk mixture, stirring to dissolve. Strain through a fine sieve into a bowl and cool.

Fold the whipped cream into the cooled milk mixture. Pour into eight 200ml dariole moulds, then chill for at least 4 hours or overnight to set.

For the poached quinces, preheat the oven to 160°C. Place quinces in a 2 litre baking dish. Combine sugar, spices, lemon rind and vanilla pod and seeds in a saucepan with 1.25 litres (5 cups) water, stirring over low heat until the sugar dissolves. Pour over the quinces, cover with foil, then bake for 3-4 hours until the quinces are tender and a deep red colour. Transfer the quinces to a serving bowl, then pour the poaching liquid into a saucepan over medium heat and cook for 8-10 minutes until reduced and syrupy. Pour over the quinces, then chill until ready to serve.

To unmould the panna cottas, dip the base of the dariole moulds briefly in hot water, then turn out onto plates. Dust with cinnamon, then serve with poached quinces and a little syrup. **Serves 8**

* Available from gourmet food shops.

DATE & BANANA LOAF

1 tsp bicarbonate of soda
300g sour cream
100ml thickened cream
125g unsalted butter, melted,
   cooled, plus extra softened
   butter to serve
250g caster sugar
2 eggs, lightly beaten
2 cups (300g) plain flour
1 tsp ground cinnamon
1 tsp baking powder
2 large over-ripe bananas,
   mashed
1/2 cup (80g) pitted chopped
   dates
1/4 cup (20g) flaked almonds
Honey, to serve

Preheat the oven to 180°C. Grease and line
a 28cm x 12cm loaf pan with baking paper.

Whisk the bicarbonate of soda and sour cream
together in a bowl and stand for 5 minutes.

Add the thickened cream, cooled butter, sugar and
egg to the sour cream mixture and stir to combine.
Sift in the flour, cinnamon and baking powder, stirring
to combine, then stir in mashed banana and dates.

Pour mixture into the loaf pan and sprinkle with
almonds. Bake for 1 hour or until a skewer inserted
into the centre comes out clean (cover loosely with
foil if browning too quickly). Cool the loaf in the pan
for 10 minutes, then transfer to a wire rack to cool.

Serve the date and banana loaf warm or cool
with butter and honey. **Serves 8**

RED WINE PEAR & ALMOND CAKE

1¹/₂ cups (375ml) red wine

300g caster sugar

2 cinnamon quills

3 firm pears (such as beurre bosc), peeled, cored, cut into thin wedges

150g unsalted butter

3 eggs

¹/₂ cup (75g) plain flour, sifted

150g almond meal

1¹/₂ tsp baking powder

Place the red wine and 150g sugar in a saucepan over low heat, stirring until the sugar dissolves. Add the cinnamon and pears, then cover the surface closely with a piece of baking paper cut to fit and cook for 10 minutes or until the pears are tender. Set aside to cool completely in the poaching liquid.

Preheat the oven to 180°C and grease a 22cm springform cake pan.

Beat the butter and remaining 150g sugar with electric beaters until thick and pale. Add the eggs, 1 at a time, beating well after each addition. Fold in the flour, almond meal and baking powder. Set aside.

Drain the pears, reserving the poaching liquid. Arrange the pear slices in the cake pan in a circular pattern, slightly overlapping. Spread over the cake batter, smoothing the top with a spatula. Bake for 35-40 minutes until a skewer inserted into the centre comes out clean. Cool in the pan for 10 minutes.

Meanwhile, place the pear poaching liquid in a saucepan over medium-high heat and cook for 6-8 minutes until reduced and syrupy.

Invert cake onto a serving plate. Brush the warm cake with the poaching syrup. Serve warm or cool.

Serves 6-8

CHEAT'S CHOCOLATE CARAMEL TARTS

Chocolate and caramel is always a popular combination, but a little sprinkling of sea salt will raise these tarts to another level. You can make all the elements yourself, or cheat with shop-bought chocolate pastry and dulce de leche.

1 quantity chocolate pastry
    (see Extras, p 246) or use
    300g packet Careme Dark
    Chocolate Shortcrust Pastry*
200g good-quality dark
    chocolate, chopped
450g jar dulce de leche*
    (or see Extras, p 246)

Preheat the oven to 180°C. Lightly grease six 10cm loose-bottomed tart pans.

Roll out the pastry to 5mm thick if using homemade. Use the pastry to line the tart pans, trimming the excess. Chill the tart shells for 10 minutes.

Line the tart shells with baking paper and fill with pastry weights or uncooked rice, then bake for 7 minutes. Remove the paper and weights, then return to the oven for a further 2 minutes or until the pastry is crisp and dry. Cool completely in the pans.

Place the chocolate in a heatproof bowl over a saucepan of gently simmering water (don't let the bowl touch the water), stirring until melted and smooth. Remove from heat and cool slightly.

Use a palette knife to spread the dulce de leche in the tart shells, then pour over the chocolate, gently swirling the tart to completely cover the caramel. Cool at room temperature until set.

Once set, sprinkle each tart with sea salt flakes and serve. **Makes 6**

* Careme pastry is available from delis and gourmet food shops; for stockists, visit: caremepastry.com. Dulce de leche is a South American milk caramel available from gourmet food shops.

WALNUT SEMIFREDDO WITH POMEGRANATE SYRUP

180g caster sugar
3/4 cup (75g) walnuts
3 eggs
600ml thickened cream,
  whipped to soft peaks
75g white chocolate,
  melted, cooled
2 tbs chopped pistachios
Pomegranate seeds (optional),
  to serve

Pomegranate syrup
200g caster sugar
50ml glucose syrup*
1 tbs pomegranate molasses*

Begin this recipe a day ahead.

Line a baking tray with a piece of lightly greased foil and line a 1 litre loaf pan with plastic wrap, leaving plenty overhanging the sides.

Place 100g sugar and 2 tablespoons water in a saucepan over low heat, stirring until the sugar dissolves. Increase heat to medium-low and cook, swirling the pan occasionally, for a further 3-4 minutes until a golden caramel. Add the walnuts, swirling the pan to coat in the caramel, then pour onto the tray and cool until hardened and set. Cut into small pieces or pulse in a food processor to make a praline.

Meanwhile, place eggs and remaining 80g sugar in a bowl set over a saucepan of simmering water (don't let the bowl touch the water) and whisk until thick and pale. Remove from the heat, then sit in a larger bowl filled with iced water (don't let any water splash into the egg mixture) and continue to whisk until cooled.

Add the whipped cream and melted chocolate to the cooled egg mixture and fold in the walnut praline. Pour into the loaf pan, cover with the overhanging plastic wrap and freeze overnight.

For the syrup, place sugar, glucose and 1/4 cup (60ml) water in a saucepan over low heat, stirring until sugar dissolves. Increase the heat to medium and cook, swirling the pan occasionally, for 5-6 minutes until a light golden caramel. Add pomegranate molasses and 2 tablespoons water, stirring until smooth. Cool.

Cut the semifreddo into slices and drizzle with the pomegranate syrup. Scatter with the pistachios and pomegranate seeds, if desired, and serve. **Serves 6-8**

* Glucose syrup is available from the baking aisle in supermarkets. Pomegranate molasses is from delis and gourmet food shops.

HONEY POTS DE CREME

$^1/_2$ cup (180g) honey,
   plus extra to serve
300ml pure (thin) cream
1 cup (250ml) milk
2 tbs caster sugar
1 vanilla bean, split,
   seeds scraped
1 egg, plus 5 extra egg yolks
Honeycomb and melted
   dark chocolate, to serve

Preheat oven to 160°C.

Place the honey, cream and milk in a saucepan over medium heat, stirring to combine. Bring to just below boiling point, then remove from heat and set aside.

Meanwhile, beat the sugar, vanilla seeds, egg and extra egg yolks with electric beaters until thick and pale. Pour the milk mixture into the egg mixture and gently stir to combine, trying not to create too much froth. Strain the mixture into a jug, then pour into six $^3/_4$ cup (185ml) ramekins or ovenproof jars.

Place ramekins in a deep roasting pan and pour enough boiling water into the pan to come halfway up the sides of the ramekins. Bake for 50-60 minutes until set but with a slight wobble. Allow to cool completely, then chill for 1 hour.

Drizzle honey pots with extra honey and serve with honeycomb dipped in melted chocolate. **Serves 6**

BOOZY AUTUMN TARTS

400g mixed dried fruit (such
   as fig, apple and pear)
100ml brandy
1 cup (220g) caster sugar
2 tbs toasted walnuts, crushed
1 egg, lightly beaten
Custard (see Extras, p 246),
   to serve

Pastry

2 cups (300g) plain flour
1/4 cup (35g) icing sugar,
   plus extra to serve
1/4 tsp baking powder
125g chilled unsalted butter,
   chopped
3 tsp lemon juice
1 egg, plus 2 extra yolks

Begin this recipe a day ahead.

Place the dried fruit in a bowl with the brandy and just enough boiling water to cover. Allow to cool, then cover and chill overnight.

The next day, for the pastry, place the flour, icing sugar and baking powder in a food processor and whiz to combine. Add the butter and whiz until the mixture resembles breadcrumbs. Add the lemon juice, egg and extra yolks, then whiz until the mixture just comes together. Shape into a ball, then enclose in plastic wrap and chill for 30 minutes.

Preheat the oven to 180°C and line a baking tray with baking paper.

Strain the dried fruit, reserving the soaking liquid. Place the soaking liquid and caster sugar in a saucepan over medium-high heat and cook, stirring occasionally, for 5-6 minutes until reduced and syrupy. Roughly chop the fruit and place in a bowl with half the syrup, reserving the remaining syrup. Set aside.

Divide pastry into 4 portions, then roll out each portion on a lightly floured surface into a 15cm circle. Place pastry circles on the baking tray, then scatter each with the crushed walnuts, leaving a 3cm border. Pile the soaked fruit on the walnuts, then fold the pastry edge over the filling, pleating and pinching together. Brush the pastry with beaten egg, then bake for 30 minutes or until pastry is golden.

Brush the warm tarts with the reserved syrup, dust with icing sugar, then serve immediately with custard.
Serves 4

BLACKBERRY FROZEN YOGHURT WITH BERRY CARAMEL

150g fresh or frozen, thawed
    blackberries
395g can sweetened
    condensed milk
500g thick Greek-style
    yoghurt

Berry caramel
1 cup (220g) caster sugar
100g fresh or frozen, thawed
    blackberries
1 tsp vanilla extract

Place the blackberries in a food processor and whiz until a smooth puree. Stir in the condensed milk and yoghurt, then transfer to an ice cream machine and churn according to the manufacturer's instructions. (Alternatively, pour the mixture into a shallow container and freeze for 2 hours or until frozen at the edges. Remove from the freezer and beat with electric beaters, then return to the freezer. Repeat the process 2-3 times.) Freeze for 3-4 hours until firm.

Meanwhile, for the blackberry caramel, place the sugar and 2 tablespoons water in a saucepan over low heat, stirring until the sugar dissolves. Increase heat to medium-high and cook, swirling the pan occasionally, for a further 3-4 minutes until a light caramel. Cool slightly. Place the blackberries and vanilla in a cleaned food processor and whiz until smooth, then stir into the caramel and allow to cool completely.

Serve the frozen blackberry yoghurt drizzled with the berry caramel. **Serves 6-8**

AUTUMN MENUS

76

90

116

78

96

118

in season

apples artichokes asian greens potatoes
beans (broad, flat, snake) beetroot broccoli
~~iflower~~ celeriac citrus fruits fennel
parsnips pears pumpkin
swede witlof

WINTER

PORCINI & CHICKEN LIVER PATE

These little pots of pâté are great to have on hand for when friends drop by and will keep in the fridge for up to 1 week.

20g dried porcini mushrooms*
450g chicken livers, cleaned, trimmed
1 cup (250ml) milk
150g unsalted butter, softened
1 red onion, finely chopped
2 garlic cloves, finely chopped
2 tsp chopped thyme leaves
2 pancetta slices, chopped
2 tbs brandy
210g jar redcurrant jelly
Baguette, to serve

Place porcini in a bowl with $1/2$ cup (125ml) boiling water and soak for 30 minutes. Place the chicken livers in a bowl, cover with the milk and soak for 30 minutes – this will result in a milder flavour.

Drain the porcini, reserving the soaking liquid, and chop. Drain livers, discarding the milk, and set aside.

Melt 25g butter in a frypan over medium heat. Cook the onion, garlic, thyme, chopped porcini and soaking liquid, stirring, for 3-4 minutes until liquid evaporates. Season, then remove from the pan and set aside.

Add 25g butter to the frypan and increase heat to medium-high. Cook livers and pancetta, turning, for 3-4 minutes until livers are browned on the outside, but still pink in the middle. Add the brandy and cook for 1 minute, then return onion mixture to the frypan, stirring to combine. Remove from the heat and cool.

Whiz liver mixture in a blender with remaining 100g butter until smooth. Press the pâté through a sieve, then spoon into four 1 cup (250ml) ramekins or jars. Cover, then chill for 30 minutes or until firm.

Melt the redcurrant jelly in a small saucepan over low heat. Cool slightly, then pour over the pâté and chill for at least 1 hour or until set. Remove from the fridge 30 minutes before serving.

Bring the pâtés back to room temperature, then serve with crusty baguette. **Serves 4**

* From gourmet food shops and greengrocers.

CURRIED CARROT & LENTIL SOUP

20g unsalted butter

2 tbs olive oil

1 onion, chopped

1 leek (white part only), chopped

2 tsp mild curry powder

1 tsp ground cumin

2 garlic cloves, chopped

$1/3$ cup (80ml) tomato passata (sugo)

1 tbs tomato paste

5 carrots, chopped

1 cup (200g) red lentils

1L (4 cups) chicken or vegetable stock

1 cup (250ml) coconut milk, plus extra to serve

Lime juice, to taste

2 tbs sunflower oil

12 fresh curry leaves*

Pappadams, to serve

Place the butter and olive oil in a saucepan over medium heat. Cook the onion and leek, stirring, for 2-3 minutes until softened, but not coloured. Add the curry powder and cumin, then cook, stirring, for 1 minute or until fragrant. Add garlic, tomato passata, tomato paste, carrot, lentils and stock, then season. Cover and simmer for 20 minutes or until the carrot is tender. Remove the soup from the heat, then use a stick blender to puree until smooth. (Alternatively, cool slightly, then puree in batches in a blender. Return to the saucepan.)

Add the coconut milk and lime juice to the soup, then gently reheat over low heat.

Meanwhile, place the sunflower oil in a small frypan over medium-high heat. Fry the curry leaves for 30 seconds or until crisp, then drain on paper towel.

Ladle the soup into bowls and drizzle with extra coconut milk. Top with fried curry leaves, then serve with pappadams. **Serves 6**

* From greengrocers and selected supermarkets.

MUSHROOM & POTATO TARTS

20g dried porcini mushrooms*
1 quantity shortcrust pastry
  (see Extras, p 246) or
  3 frozen, thawed shortcrust
  pastry sheets
2 potatoes (about 400g),
  peeled
2 eggs
1 cup (240g) creme fraiche
2 tsp chopped thyme leaves
$1/4$ cup (65g) goat's cheese,
  crumbled
30g unsalted butter
1 tbs olive oil
1 garlic clove, finely chopped
300g mixed fresh mushrooms
  (such as Swiss brown and
  chestnut), sliced if large
2 tbs chopped flat-leaf parsley
Salad leaves, to serve

Soak the dried porcini in $1/2$ cup (125ml) boiling water for 30 minutes. Drain, squeezing out excess liquid, then roughly chop porcini and set aside.

Roll out the pastry to 5mm thick if using homemade. Use the pastry to line six 12cm loose-bottomed tart pans, trimming any excess. Chill for 15 minutes.

Place the potatoes in a saucepan of cold, salted water. Bring to the boil over medium-high heat, then cook for 8-10 minutes to par-boil. Cool, then slice into thin rounds.

Preheat the oven to 180°C.

Line the tart shells with baking paper and fill with pastry weights or uncooked rice. Bake for 10 minutes, then remove paper and weights and bake for a further 2-3 minutes or until golden and dry. Cool slightly.

Whisk the eggs, creme fraiche and 1 teaspoon thyme together, then season. Arrange the potato slices, slightly overlapping, in the tart shells and pour over the creme fraiche mixture. Scatter with the goat's cheese and bake for 15 minutes or until filling is set.

Meanwhile, place the butter and oil in a frypan over medium-high heat. Add the garlic, fresh mushrooms and remaining 1 teaspoon thyme, then cook, stirring, for 3-4 minutes until softened. Add the porcini and parsley, then season and cook for a further 2-3 minutes until tender.

Top the tarts with the mushroom mixture and serve with salad leaves. **Serves 6**

* Available from delis and gourmet food shops.

SINGAPORE NOODLES

This is a regular midweek meal in my house. The trick is to have all your ingredients chopped and ready, then you just toss everything together in the wok.

50g dried shiitake
    mushrooms*
2 tbs dried shrimp*
400g fresh Singapore noodles
1 cup (120g) frozen peas
1 tbs peanut oil
1 onion, thinly sliced
1 carrot, cut into matchsticks
1 red capsicum, thinly sliced
1 tbs mild curry powder
250g Chinese barbecue pork*,
    chopped
200g small cooked,
    peeled prawns
2 tbs Chinese rice wine
    (shaohsing)*
2 tbs kecap manis (Indonesian
    sweet soy sauce)*
4 spring onions, thinly sliced
    on an angle
Coriander leaves, to serve

Place the shiitake and dried shrimp in a bowl, cover with boiling water, then allow to soak for 15 minutes. Drain, reserving the soaking liquid. Halve the shiitake if large and set aside.

Meanwhile, place noodles and peas in a large bowl, cover with boiling water, and soak for 5 minutes. Drain, then gently separate noodles and set aside.

Heat the oil in a wok over medium-high heat. Add the onion, carrot, capsicum and curry powder, then cook, stirring, for 1-2 minutes until the vegetables have started to soften. Add the pork, prawns, rice wine, kecap manis, noodles, peas, shiitake, soaked shrimp, 1/4 cup (60ml) reserved soaking liquid and half the spring onion, then stir-fry for 2-3 minutes until warmed through.

Divide Singapore noodles among bowls, then serve garnished with coriander and remaining spring onion.
Serves 4-6

* Dried shiitake mushrooms, dried shrimp, Chinese rice wine and kecap manis are available from Asian food shops. Chinese barbecue pork is available from Asian barbecue shops.

POTATO 'TACOS' WITH TOMATO SALSA

The homemade tomato salsa for these potato skin 'tacos' is also wonderful with burgers and sandwiches. It will keep in the fridge in an airtight container for up to 1 week.

8 desiree potatoes (unpeeled)
1 tbs olive oil
25g unsalted butter
$1/2$ tsp smoked paprika
   (pimenton)
Guacamole (see Extras, p 246)
   and sour cream, to serve

Tomato salsa
400g can chopped tomatoes
2 eschalots, chopped
100g brown sugar
$1/3$ cup (80ml) white
   wine vinegar
$1/2$ tsp smoked paprika
   (pimenton)

Preheat the oven to 200°C. Line a baking tray with baking paper.

Prick the potatoes with a fork, then place on the baking tray and drizzle with oil. Bake for 1-$1^1/2$ hours until tender. Cool, halve, then scoop out and discard the soft potato centre, reserving the potato skins – these will become your 'taco' shells.

Meanwhile, for the tomato salsa, place all the ingredients in a saucepan and bring to the boil. Reduce heat to low, season, then simmer, stirring occasionally, for 25-30 minutes until thick. Cool slightly.

Place the butter and paprika in a small saucepan over low heat and cook until melted and combined. Toss the potato skins in the paprika butter, then place, cut-side up, on a baking paper-lined baking tray and bake for a further 15 minutes or until crisp.

Serve the potato 'tacos' with guacamole, sour cream and warm tomato salsa. **Serves 4**

ASIAN STEAK TARTARE WITH WONTON CRISPS

8 wonton wrappers*
Sunflower oil, to shallow-fry
300g good-quality beef rump
   or eye-fillet steak, trimmed,
   very finely chopped
4 quail egg yolks*
Micro herbs or extra coriander
   leaves and fried Asian
   shallots*, to serve

Dressing
2 tsp sunflower oil
1 tbs finely chopped coriander
1 tbs finely chopped
   Vietnamese* or regular mint
2 tbs fish sauce
2 tsp caster sugar
2 tsp finely grated lime zest,
   plus 1½ tsp lime juice
2 tsp rice vinegar
1 tsp sriracha chilli sauce*
   or chilli jam*

Using scissors, cut the wonton wrappers in half on the diagonal. Heat 2cm oil in a small saucepan. In batches, shallow-fry the wonton wrapper halves for 30 seconds or until puffed and crisp. Drain the wonton crisps on paper towel. Set aside.

For the dressing, place all the ingredients in a bowl and whisk to combine. Taste, then adjust the flavours as needed – there should be a balance of salty, hot, sour and sweet.

Add the chopped steak to the dressing and mix well to combine. Place an egg ring on each serving plate, then divide the steak mixture among the egg rings. Make a small indent in the top of the steak mixture using the back of a teaspoon, then carefully place an egg yolk in each indent. Carefully remove the egg rings, then scatter with herbs and fried shallots. Serve immediately with wonton crisps.

Serves 4

* Available from Asian food shops.

RADICCHIO & GORGONZOLA RISOTTO

1L (4 cups) chicken or
    vegetable stock
2 cups (500ml) dry white wine
60g unsalted butter
$1/3$ cup (80ml) olive oil
1 onion, finely chopped
2 garlic cloves, thinly sliced
400g arborio rice
2 bay leaves
1 radicchio, outer leaves
    discarded, inner leaves
    roughly torn
$1^3/4$ cups (140g) finely grated
    parmesan, plus extra to serve
2 tbs chopped flat-leaf
    parsley leaves
150g gorgonzola dolce or
    other mild creamy blue
    cheese, crumbled

Place the stock and wine in a saucepan and bring to the boil, then keep warm over low heat.

Place the butter and oil in a deep frypan over medium-low heat. Add the onion and garlic and cook, stirring, for 2-3 minutes until softened. Add the rice and bay leaves and cook, stirring, for 2 minutes to coat the grains.

Stir in the stock mixture, a ladleful at a time, allowing each to be absorbed before adding the next. Continue to cook, stirring frequently, until all the stock has been absorbed and the rice is al dente – this should take about 20 minutes.

Fold through the radicchio, parmesan, parsley and half the gorgonzola, then stand for 2 minutes or until the cheese has melted and the radicchio has wilted slightly.

Divide risotto among plates, then serve scattered with the remaining gorgonzola and extra parmesan.

Serves 6

CRISPY POLENTA WITH TRUFFLED MUSHROOMS AND TALEGGIO

My weekly visits to the farmers' market often result in me coming home with bags full of wild mushrooms. I pair them with crispy polenta for the perfect winter warmer.

2 cups (500ml) chicken or
    vegetable stock
1/2 cup (85g) instant polenta
1 cup (80g) finely grated
    parmesan
30g unsalted butter, chopped
1/2 cup (125ml) olive oil
350g mixed mushrooms
    (such as chestnut and king
    brown), sliced if large
2 garlic cloves, finely chopped
1 tbs chopped thyme leaves
1 tbs chopped tarragon leaves
1 tbs truffle oil*,
    plus extra to serve
100g Taleggio or other soft
    washed-rind cheese, rind
    removed, chopped
Chopped flat-leaf parsley
    leaves, to serve

Place the stock in a saucepan over medium-high heat. Bring to the boil, then reduce heat to low. Pour in the polenta in a slow, steady stream and cook, stirring constantly, for 2-3 minutes until thick. Stir in the parmesan and butter, season, then pour into a lightly oiled 16cm x 10cm plastic container or baking pan. Cool, then chill for 30 minutes or until firm. Cut the polenta into eight 8cm long rectangles.

Heat 1/3 cup (80ml) olive oil in a frypan over medium-high heat. In batches, fry the polenta for 2-3 minutes each side until a golden crust forms. Keep warm.

Wipe the frypan clean with paper towel, then add the remaining 2 tablespoons olive oil and place over high heat. In 2 batches, pan-fry the mushrooms for 2-3 minutes until just starting to soften. Return all the mushrooms to the pan with the garlic, thyme, tarragon and truffle oil, season, then cook, stirring, for a further 1 minute.

Divide the polenta among plates, top with the mushroom mixture and dot with the Taleggio, allowing it to melt slightly. Sprinkle with parsley, drizzle with extra truffle oil and serve. **Serves 4**

* Truffle oil is from delis and gourmet food shops; substitute extra virgin olive oil.

POACHED CHICKEN WITH WARM ASIAN VINAIGRETTE

4 x 170g chicken breast fillets
1 jasmine green tea bag
1 cup (200g) jasmine rice
1/2 cup (125ml) rice wine
    vinegar
1/4 cup (60ml) soy sauce
1/4 cup (60ml) mirin
    (Japanese rice wine)*
1/4 cup (60g) grated dark palm
    sugar* or dark brown sugar
2 tbs sesame oil
3cm piece ginger, cut into
    very thin matchsticks
1 cup shredded spring onions
Micro herbs or coriander
    leaves, to serve

Place the chicken in a saucepan, cover completely with cold water and 1 teaspoon salt, then bring to the boil. Cover, then remove from heat and stand for 30 minutes or until chicken is cooked through.

Meanwhile, place the tea bag in a saucepan with 2 1/2 cups (625ml) boiling water. Remove from the heat, then allow to steep for 15 minutes. Remove the tea bag, then add 1 teaspoon salt and bring back to the boil. Add the rice and cook according to the packet instructions, then drain.

Place the vinegar, soy sauce, mirin, sugar and sesame oil in a small saucepan over medium-low heat, stirring to dissolve the sugar. Stir in the ginger and 1/2 cup spring onion, then remove from heat.

Remove the chicken from the poaching liquid and thickly slice. Spoon the jasmine rice onto plates, top with the chicken and drizzle with warm vinaigrette. Garnish with herbs and the remaining 1/2 cup spring onion, then serve. **Serves 4**

* Available from selected supermarkets and Asian food shops.

TOAD IN THE HOLE WITH MUSTARD & ONION GRAVY

3/4 cup (110g) plain flour,
  sifted, plus 1 tbs extra
3 eggs
300ml milk
1 tbs finely chopped chives
1 tbs finely chopped flat-leaf
  parsley leaves
2 tbs sunflower oil
8 pork chipolata sausages
1 large red onion,
  cut into thin wedges
1 tbs wholegrain mustard
2 tbs thyme leaves
300ml beef stock
1 tsp Worcestershire sauce
1 tbs redcurrant jelly
1/2 tsp tomato paste

Preheat oven to 180°C.

Place the flour, eggs, milk, chives, parsley and 1 teaspoon salt in a bowl and whisk to combine. Stand the batter for 15 minutes.

Place 1 tablespoon oil in a frypan over medium-high heat. Cook the chipolatas, turning, for 4-5 minutes until well browned and almost cooked through.

Remove chipolatas from the pan and roughly chop. Divide the chipolatas and any oil from the frypan among four 1½ cup (375ml) pie dishes (or use eight holes of 2 Texas muffin pans). Pour in the batter, filling the pie dishes or muffin holes to three-quarters full. Bake for 20 minutes or until puffed and golden.

Meanwhile, place the remaining 1 tablespoon oil in the frypan and place over medium heat. Add the onion to the pan and cook, stirring occasionally, for 3-4 minutes until soft and golden. Sprinkle the extra 1 tablespoon flour over the onion, stirring to combine, then add the mustard, thyme, stock, Worcestershire, redcurrant jelly and tomato paste. Cook, whisking occasionally, for 3-4 minutes until thickened.

Serve the toad in the hole immediately with the mustard and onion gravy. **Serves 4**

ROAST QUAIL WITH SPLIT PEA DHAL

2 tbs sunflower oil
1 tsp ground cardamom
1 tsp ground cumin
Pinch of cayenne pepper
6 quails*, butterflied (ask
    your butcher to do this)
150g green beans, blanched
Curry butter (see Extras,
    p 246) and coriander
    sprigs, to serve

Split pea dhal
300g dried yellow split peas
2 tbs sunflower oil
1 onion, finely chopped
1 tbs panch phoran
    (Indian spice mix)*

For the dhal, soak the split peas in cold water for 2 hours, then drain. Place the oil in a saucepan over low heat. Cook the onion, stirring, for 2-3 minutes until softened. Stir in the panch phoran, then add the split peas and 3 cups (750ml) water. Bring to a simmer, then reduce heat to low and cook, stirring occasionally, for 1-1¼ hours until the split peas are soft, topping up with more water if the mixture becomes too dry. Beat with a wooden spoon, then season and keep warm.

Meanwhile, preheat the oven to 190°C.

Rub the oil and spices over the quails, then season. In batches, cook the quails, skin-side down, in a frypan over medium-high heat for 2-3 minutes until starting to brown. Transfer the quails a baking tray, skin-side up, and roast for 8 minutes or until just cooked. Rest, loosely covered with foil, for 5 minutes.

Pile the dhal onto plates and top with beans and quail. Top quail with a slice of curry butter and serve garnished with coriander. **Serves 6**

* Quail is from selected butchers and poultry shops. Panch phoran is a mixture of fennel, cumin, nigella, fenugreek and mustard seeds, available from Indian food shops and Herbie's Spices (herbies.com.au).

ASIAN-STYLE OSSO BUCO

1 tsp five-spice powder
1/4 cup (35g) plain flour
6 x 4cm pieces veal shin
　(osso buco)
2 tbs sunflower oil
2 onions, chopped
3cm piece ginger, grated
2 garlic cloves, finely chopped
2 strips pared orange zest
3 star anise
1 cinnamon quill
1/3 firmly packed cup
　(80g) brown sugar
1/2 cup (125ml) soy sauce
2 tbs char sui sauce (Chinese
　barbecue sauce)*
1 tbs tomato paste
1L (4 cups) beef consommé
　or stock
1/2 cup coriander leaves
1/2 cup mint leaves
2 spring onions, shredded
1 long red chilli, seeds
　removed, thinly sliced
Juice of 1/2 lime
Steamed rice, to serve

Preheat the oven to 170°C.

Combine the five-spice and flour in a bowl. Coat the meat in the flour mixture, shaking off and reserving any excess flour.

Place 1 tablespoon oil in an ovenproof casserole over medium heat. In batches, cook the meat for 1-2 minutes each side until golden. Remove from the pan and set aside.

Add the remaining 1 tablespoon oil to the pan. Add the onion, ginger and garlic, then cook for 2-3 minutes until softened. Add the orange zest, star anise, cinnamon, sugar, soy sauce, char sui sauce, tomato paste, consommé or stock and reserved flour mixture, then return the meat to the pan and stir to combine. (Make sure the meat is completely covered in liquid, adding more stock or water if necessary.) Bring to a simmer, then cover and transfer to the oven. Bake for 2 hours or until the meat is tender.

Just before serving, place the coriander, mint, spring onion and chilli in a bowl, then toss with the lime juice to combine.

Spoon the meat and sauce onto plates, top with the herb salad and serve with steamed rice. **Serves 6**

* Available from selected supermarkets and Asian food shops.

PORK & FENNEL TRAY BAKE WITH MOROCCAN SPICE

2 x 400g pork fillets, trimmed,
   cut into thirds
3 large potatoes,
   cut into wedges
3 small fennel bulbs, trimmed,
   cut into quarters
3 red onions, cut into quarters
1 tbs olive oil
Thick Greek-style yoghurt,
   seasoned with salt and
   pepper, to serve

Marinade
2 preserved lemon quarters*,
   flesh and white pith
   removed, rind thinly sliced
1 garlic clove, chopped
1 small red chilli, seeds
   removed, chopped
1 tsp smoked paprika
   (pimenton)
1 tsp ground cumin
1 tbs honey
1 cup coriander leaves,
   plus extra to serve
1/4 cup (60ml) olive oil

Preheat the oven to 190°C and grease a large roasting pan.

For the marinade, place all the ingredients in a small food processor, season, then whiz into a paste. Coat the pork in the paste, then set aside to marinate while you prepare the vegetables.

Place the potato and fennel in a saucepan of cold, salted water. Bring to the boil over medium heat, then cook for 5 minutes to par-boil. Drain, then place in the roasting pan with the onion. Drizzle with the oil, season, then roast for 20 minutes or until just tender.

Add the pork to the roasting pan and toss well with the vegetables. Roast for 20-25 minutes until the pork is cooked. Transfer the pork to a plate and rest, loosely covered with foil, for 10 minutes.

Increase the oven to 220°C.

Return the vegetables to the oven for a further 10 minutes or until caramelised and crisp.

Serve the vegetables with the pork, seasoned yoghurt and extra coriander leaves. **Serves 4-6**

* Available from delis and gourmet food shops.

THAI BEEF CURRY WITH HOLY BASIL

2 tbs sunflower oil
8 Asian (red) eschalots*,
   thinly sliced
400g beef fillet, cut into
   very thin strips
2 tbs Thai red curry paste
400ml can coconut milk
1/2 cup (75g) roasted
   peanuts, crushed,
   plus extra to serve
2 tbs grated palm sugar*
3 kaffir lime leaves*,
   plus extra shredded
   kaffir lime leaves to serve
1/4 cup (60ml) fish sauce
1 cup Thai basil leaves*
   or regular basil leaves,
   plus extra to serve
Juice of 1/2 lime
Sliced red chilli, bean spouts
   and steamed rice, to serve

Heat 1 tablespoon oil in a wok over high heat. Stir-fry half the eschalot for 30 seconds or until softened. Remove from tne wok and set aside.

Add the remaining 1 tablespoon oil to the wok. In 3 batches, stir-fry the beef for 1-2 minutes until browned. Remove from the wok and set aside.

Add the curry paste and 100ml coconut milk to the wok, reduce the heat to medium-high and cook, stirring, for 1-2 minutes until fragrant and the oil has separated from the milk. Add the remaining 300ml coconut milk and simmer for 5 minutes. Add the peanuts, sugar and kaffir lime leaves and simmer for 5 minutes, then return the beef and cooked eschalot to the wok with the fish sauce. Cook for a further 30 seconds, then remove the wok from the heat and stir through the basil and lime juice.

Garnish curry with chilli, bean sprouts, shredded kaffir lime leaves, remaining eschalot and extra peanuts and basil. Serve with steamed rice. **Serves 4**

* Available from Asian food shops.

CHORIZO-CRUSTED BLUE-EYE WITH SPICED BEANS

4 x 180g skinless blue-eye
  fillets
1 tbs olive oil
1 onion, finely chopped
1 tsp ground cumin
1/2 tsp ground turmeric
1 tsp smoked paprika
  (pimenton)
1 tbs tomato paste
400g can chopped tomatoes
1/4 cup (55g) caster sugar
100ml red wine vinegar
2 x 400g cans cannellini beans,
  rinsed, drained
Salad leaves and lemon
  wedges, to serve

Chorizo crust
1 dried chorizo sausage,
  casing removed, roughly
  chopped
1 1/4 cups (105g) fresh
  sourdough breadcrumbs
20g unsalted butter
1 garlic clove, chopped
2 tbs chopped flat-leaf
  parsley leaves
1/2 tsp smoked paprika
  (pimenton)

Preheat the oven to 200°C and line a baking tray with baking paper.

For the chorizo crust, place all the ingredients in a food processor and whiz until well combined.

Season the fish, then pat the chorizo mixture on top. Place on the baking tray and chill for 10 minutes.

Meanwhile, place the oil in a frypan over low heat. Add the onion and cook, stirring, for 2-3 minutes until softened. Add the cumin, turmeric and paprika, then cook, stirring, for 1 minute or until fragrant. Add the tomato paste and cook, stirring, for a further 1 minute, then add the chopped tomatoes, sugar and vinegar, stirring to dissolve the sugar. Cook for 5 minutes or until reduced by one-third. Add the beans and cook for a further 5 minutes or until slightly thickened – add a little water if the mixture is too thick. Season and keep warm.

Bake the fish for 8-10 minutes until the crust is golden and the fish is just cooked.

Serve the fish with the spiced beans, salad leaves and lemon wedges. **Serves 4**

CONFIT DUCK WITH HONEY & GINGER GLAZE

I used to think that duck was too lavish and fiddly to cook at home, but now that confit duck is more widely available, it's my go-to dish for a midweek dinner party. Just add a deceptively easy honey and ginger glaze and you have a meal that's sure to impress.

150ml white wine
2 tbs sweet chilli sauce
2 tbs honey
2cm piece ginger, grated
1 cup (250ml) chicken stock
4 pontiac potatoes, peeled,
    cut into 3cm pieces
4 confit duck legs*
Watercress sprigs, to serve

Preheat the oven to 180°C.

Place the wine in a saucepan over medium-high heat, bring to a simmer, then cook for 3-4 minutes until reduced by half. Add the sweet chilli sauce, honey, ginger and stock, then simmer for a further 3-4 minutes until syrupy. Set glaze aside.

Meanwhile, place the potatoes in a saucepan of cold, salted water. Bring to the boil over medium-high heat, then cook for 6-8 minutes to par-boil. Drain well.

Scrape excess fat from the duck legs and set legs aside. Place 2 tablespoons duck fat on a baking tray and warm in the oven for 5 minutes. Carefully toss the potatoes in the hot fat, then season and bake, turning once, for 20-25 minutes until golden.

Add the duck legs to the baking tray and brush with the glaze. Return the baking tray to the oven for 10 minutes or until the duck legs are warmed through.

Brush the duck with any remaining glaze, then divide among plates and serve with the potato and watercress. **Serves 4**

* Available from selected butchers.

LAMB & KUMARA TAGINE

I've adapted this recipe from a dish I saw Bill Granger cook on TV. It reminded me that the often overlooked chump chop is actually a wonderful cut for slow cooking. Thanks, Bill.

1 tbs olive oil
6 x 100g lamb chump chops
1 onion, thinly sliced
2cm piece ginger, grated
4 garlic cloves, finely chopped
1 tbs ras el hanout*
1 tbs harissa*
1 bunch coriander, roots and
    stems finely chopped, leaves
    reserved for couscous
400g can chopped tomatoes
800g kumara, chopped
2 tbs lemon juice
1 tbs soy sauce
2 tbs honey
2 cinnamon quills
2 cups (500ml) beef stock

Pomegranate couscous

1 cup (200g) couscous
1 tsp harissa*
1 tbs pomegranate molasses*
1 tsp ras el hanout*
Juice ½ lemon
1 small red onion, thinly sliced
Seeds of 1 pomegranate*

Preheat the oven to 180°C.

Place the oil in an ovenproof casserole over medium-high heat. Season the lamb chops and cook, in batches, for 2-3 minutes each side until browned. Remove from the pan and set aside.

Add the onion to the pan and cook, stirring, for 1-2 minutes until soft. Add the ginger, garlic, ras el hanout, harissa and coriander root and stem, then cook, stirring, for 1 minute or until fragrant. Return the lamb chops to the pan with the tomato, kumara, lemon juice, soy sauce, honey and cinnamon, stirring to combine. Add the stock and bring to a simmer, then cover and transfer to the oven to bake for 2 hours or until meat is falling off the bone.

Meanwhile, for the couscous, place couscous in a bowl with harissa, pomegranate molasses and ras el hanout, stirring to combine. Pour in 400ml boiling water, then cover and stand for 5 minutes or until water has been absorbed. Fluff with a fork, then toss with remaining ingredients and reserved coriander leaves.

Serve the tagine with the couscous. **Serves 6**

* Ras el hanout (Middle Eastern spice mix), harissa (North African chilli paste) and pomegranate molasses are from Middle Eastern food shops. Pomegranates are available in season from greengrocers.

EIGHT-HOUR PORK BELLY WITH CARAMELISED PEANUT & CHILLI RELISH

The long, slow cooking of the pork results in meat that is meltingly tender. Make sure you try it with the caramelised peanut and chilli relish for a truly delicious finish.

1.5kg boneless pork belly (skin on)
Sunflower oil, to rub
Steamed bok choy, to serve

Caramelised peanut & chilli relish
1/4 cup (60ml) peanut oil
2 garlic cloves, chopped
1 long red chilli, seeds removed, chopped
4 Asian (red) eschalots*, chopped
2 tsp caster sugar
2 tbs unsalted peanuts
1/2 tsp ground coriander
1 tbs sesame oil
1 tbs soy sauce
Juice 1 lime
2 tbs finely chopped coriander, plus extra to serve

Preheat the oven to 100°C or its lowest temperature.

Score the pork skin and fat in a criss-cross pattern, without cutting into the meat. Place pork on a rack in the sink and pour over a kettle of boiling water (this will result in crisp crackling). Dry well with paper towel, then rub the pork skin with the sunflower oil and 1 tablespoon sea salt.

Place the pork, skin-side up, on a rack set in a roasting pan and pour in 200ml water. Roast for 8 hours or until very tender.

Increase the oven to 220°C.

Roast the pork for a further 20 minutes or until the crackling is crisp.

Meanwhile, for the relish, heat 1 tablespoon peanut oil in a small frypan over medium-high heat. Cook the garlic and chilli, stirring, for 1-2 minutes until fragrant. Stir in eschalot and sugar, then cook for 3-4 minutes until the sugar starts to caramelise. Add peanuts and ground coriander, then cook, stirring, for 1-2 minutes to coat the peanuts. Transfer the mixture to a mortar and pestle and pound into a coarse paste. Stir in the remaining ingredients and 2-3 tablespoons water.

Slice the pork belly, garnish with coriander leaves and serve with the bok choy and relish. **Serves 4-6**

* From Asian food shops and selected greengrocers.

CHOCOLATE LAVA PUDDINGS

Chocolate fondant puddings, with their molten centres, are a fixture on restaurant menus – this is my cheat's version, using chocolate truffles to achieve the rich, melting centre. They taste just as good, but are completely stress-free.

250g unsalted butter, softened

1 firmly packed cup (250g) brown sugar

4 eggs

1 cup (150g) plain flour

1/2 cup (50g) cocoa powder

6 chilled chocolate truffles (such as Lindt Lindor balls)

Icing sugar and pure (thin) cream or ice cream, to serve

Preheat the oven to 180°C and grease six ³/4 cup (185ml) ramekins.

Place the butter and brown sugar in a bowl and beat with electric beaters until thick and pale. Add the eggs, 1 at a time, beating well after each addition. Sift in the flour and cocoa, then fold gently with a metal spoon until just combined.

Divide half the pudding batter among the ramekins, then place a truffle in the centre of each. Top with the remaining pudding batter, then bake for 20 minutes or until just firm to the touch.

Stand puddings for 5 minutes, then dust with icing sugar and serve with cream or ice cream. **Serves 6**

STICKY DATE TART WITH TOFFEE SAUCE

1¹/₂ cups (240g) pitted dates, chopped into small pieces
150ml milk
1 tsp bicarbonate of soda
1 quantity sweet shortcrust pastry (see Extras, p 246) or 435g packet Careme Vanilla Bean Sweet Shortcrust pastry*
1 tsp vanilla extract
²/₃ cup (100g) plain flour, sifted
2 eggs, lightly beaten
2 tbs golden syrup
100g brown sugar
¹/₄ cup (20g) flaked almonds
Icing sugar, to dust

Toffee sauce
200g brown sugar
50g unsalted butter
300ml thickened cream

Place the dates and milk in a saucepan over medium heat. Bring to just below boiling point, then remove from heat. Stir in the bicarbonate of soda, then stand for 30 minutes or until dates have softened.

Meanwhile, roll out the pastry to 5mm thick if using homemade. Use the pastry to line a greased 36cm x 12cm rectangular loose-bottomed tart pan, trimming the excess. Chill for 10 minutes.

Preheat the oven to 180°C.

Line the chilled tart case with baking paper and fill with pastry weights or uncooked rice. Bake for 8 minutes. Remove the paper and weights, then bake for a further 2-3 minutes until golden and dry.

Reduce the oven to 160°C.

Place the dates and milk in a food processor with the vanilla and pulse to combine. Transfer to a bowl, then fold in the flour, eggs, golden syrup and brown sugar until just combined. Set aside.

For the toffee sauce, place all the ingredients in a saucepan over low heat, stirring until sugar dissolves. Cook for 2 minutes or until slightly thickened.

Pour ¹/₃ cup (80ml) toffee sauce in the tart shell, then spread the date mixture on top and scatter with the almonds. Bake for 20-25 minutes until just set. Cool in the pan for 5 minutes.

Remove the sticky date tart from pan and dust with icing sugar. Cut into slices and serve warm with the remaining toffee sauce. **Serves 6**

* From delis and gourmet food shops; for stockists, visit: caremepastry.com.

COCONUT CREME CARAMEL

500g caster sugar
400ml can coconut milk
300ml pure (thin) cream
300ml milk
2 eggs, plus extra 7 egg yolks
Seasonal fruit, to serve

Begin this recipe a day ahead.

Preheat the oven to 160°C.

Place 300g sugar and 2 tablespoons cold water in a saucepan over medium-low heat, stirring until sugar dissolves. Increase the heat to medium and cook, swirling the pan occasionally, for 5-6 minutes until a golden caramel. Pour into a 20cm round cake pan (not springform).

Place the coconut milk, cream, milk and remaining 200g sugar in a saucepan over medium heat. Bring to just below boiling point, then remove from the heat.

Lightly beat the eggs and extra yolks together in a large bowl, then pour the warm milk mixture into the eggs, gently whisking to combine. Strain into a jug, then pour over the caramel.

Place the cake pan in a deep roasting pan. Fill the roasting pan with enough boiling water to come halfway up the sides of the cake pan. Loosely cover the roasting pan with foil, then bake for 1 hour – the creme caramel should still have a slight wobble, but will firm on cooling. Cool in the pan, then chill overnight.

To unmould the creme caramel, dip the base of the cake pan briefly in hot water, then carefully invert the creme caramel onto a plate. Cut into slices and serve with seasonal fruit. **Serves 6**

APPLE & PASSIONFRUIT CRUMBLE

In the depth of winter, adding a little passionfruit to desserts brings a lovely freshness and the promise of warmer times to come.

130g chilled unsalted butter, chopped
8 green apples, peeled, sliced
$^2/_3$ cup (150g) caster sugar
Pulp of 8 passionfruit
1 tsp vanilla extract
1$^1/_3$ cups (200g) plain flour
Custard (see Extras, p 246), to serve

Preheat the oven to 180°C and grease six $^3/_4$ cup (185ml) ramekins or ovenproof cups (or use a 1 litre baking dish).

Place 30g butter in a saucepan over medium-low heat. Add apple, 40g sugar and $^1/_4$ cup (60ml) water, then cook for 5-6 minutes until softened. Stir in passionfruit and vanilla, then divide among ramekins.

Place the flour and remaining $^1/_2$ cup (110g) sugar and 100g butter in a food processor and whiz to coarse crumbs. Scatter the crumbs over the apple mixture, then bake for 35-40 minutes until golden and bubbling. Serve crumble warm with custard. **Serves 6**

LITTLE MANDARIN PUDDINGS

90g caster sugar,
   plus extra to sprinkle
2 mandarins, sliced into
   rounds, plus thinly zested
   rind and juice of 1 mandarin
90g unsalted butter, softened
90g self-raising flour
1/2 tsp baking powder
2 eggs
1 1/2 tbs sour cream
1 tbs orange marmalade
1/2 tsp ground ginger
1/2 tsp ground cinnamon
2 tsp golden syrup
Pure (thin) cream or custard
   (see Extras, p 246), to serve

Mandarin syrup
1/3 cup (75g) caster sugar
Juice of 2 mandarins
2 tbs golden syrup

Preheat oven to 180°C. Grease six 1 cup (250ml) dariole moulds and sprinkle the insides with the extra caster sugar, shaking out any excess. Line the base of each dariole mould with a mandarin round.

Place the butter and sugar in a bowl and beat with electric beaters until thick and pale. Add the flour, baking powder, eggs, sour cream, marmalade, spices, golden syrup and mandarin juice, then beat for a further 2-3 minutes until combined.

Divide the pudding batter among the moulds. Place a small sheet of foil on a small sheet of baking paper, then fold a pleat through the centre. Use to cover a mould, baking paper-side down, and secure with kitchen string. Repeat for remaining moulds.

Place moulds in a roasting pan, then pour enough boiling water into the pan to come halfway up the sides of the moulds. Bake for 55-60 minutes until a skewer inserted into the centre comes out clean.

Meanwhile, place the mandarin rind in a saucepan over low heat and cover with cold water. Simmer for 10 minutes. Drain. Repeat blanching method 2 more times. (This will remove the bitterness from the rind.)

For the mandarin syrup, place the sugar, mandarin juice and golden syrup in a saucepan over low heat, stirring to dissolve the sugar. Increase heat to medium and simmer for 3-4 minutes until reduced and syrupy.

Invert the puddings onto serving plates and pour over the syrup. Garnish with the blanched mandarin rind and serve with cream or custard. **Serves 6**

BACI BISCUITS

A friend of mine shared this recipe with me that she had been given while living in the US. It's incredibly simple, but tastes incredibly good. These biscuits will keep in an airtight container for up to 3 days.

40g unsalted butter, softened
1 egg
400g jar Nutella or other
   chocolate hazelnut spread
1¼ cups (185g) self-raising
   flour, sifted
Cocoa powder, to serve

Preheat the oven to 180°C. Line 2 large baking trays with baking paper.

Place the butter, egg and ³/₄ cup (235g) Nutella in a bowl and beat with electric beaters for 2-3 minutes until thick. Gradually add the flour, beating constantly, until you have a sticky dough.

Using floured hands, roll 1 teaspoon dough into a ball. Repeat until you have 50 balls. Place on the baking trays, spaced 2cm apart, and bake for 6-7 minutes until firm to the touch. Transfer to a wire rack to cool completely.

Spread the remaining Nutella on 25 biscuits, then sandwich with the remaining 25 biscuits. Serve dusted with cocoa. **Makes 25**

POACHED PEARS WITH SWEET LABNE AND SPICED CRUMBS

600g caster sugar

750ml rosé wine

6 cardamom pods

1 cinnamon quill

3 star anise

Finely grated zest of 1 lemon

2 vanilla beans, split,
    seeds scraped

6 firm pears (such as beurre
    bosc) peeled, halved, cored
    (stalks intact)

Sweet labne

1$1/2$ cups (420g) thick
    Greek-style yoghurt

$1/4$ cup (35g) icing sugar, sifted

Pinch of ground cinnamon

Spiced crumbs

3 rye bread slices

$1/2$ cup (75g) hazelnuts,
    toasted, skins removed

$1/3$ firmly packed cup (80g)
    brown sugar

1 tsp ground cloves

1 tsp ground cinnamon

Make the sweet labne a day ahead.

For the labne, line a sieve with muslin or a clean Chux and place over a bowl. Place all the ingredients in a bowl and stir well to combine, then transfer to the sieve. Draw up the sides of the muslin to make a tight parcel, then secure with kitchen string. Place in the fridge and allow to drain for 24 hours or until firm.

The next day, preheat the oven to 180°C.

For the spiced crumbs, place the bread on a baking tray and bake for 10-15 minutes until crisp and dry. Cool, then place the bread in a food processor with the hazelnuts, brown sugar and spices. Whiz to coarse crumbs.

Meanwhile, place the caster sugar, wine, spices, lemon zest and vanilla pod and seeds in a large saucepan over medium-low heat, stirring to dissolve the sugar. Add the pears, cover the surface closely with a piece of baking paper cut to fit, then simmer for 12-15 minutes until pears soften but still hold their shape (the cooking time will depend on the ripeness of the pears). Remove the pears from the pan with a slotted spoon and arrange on a serving platter.

Return the saucepan to medium-high heat, then simmer for 8-10 minutes until reduced by half.

Pour the poaching syrup over the pears and serve with the spiced crumbs and sweet labne. **Serves 6**

PERSIAN TRIFLE

These exotic desserts are surprisingly easy to prepare, and with flavours of rosewater and Turkish delight, they will transport you to a far off place from the very first mouthful.

2 tbs Cointreau or other
   orange liqueur
Finely grated zest and juice
   of 1 orange
Finely grated zest and juice
   of 1 lemon
1/2 cup (75g) icing sugar, sifted
300g plain sponge cake
   (or see Extras, p 246),
   cut into 2cm pieces
12 pieces (240g) Turkish
   delight, chopped
1 tbs rosewater*
300ml carton thick custard
300ml thickened cream
250g thick Greek-style
   yoghurt
Juice and seeds of
   1 pomegranate* (optional)
Edible dried rose petals*
   and chopped pistachios
   (optional), to serve

Place the Cointreau, orange and lemon zest and juice, and 1/4 cup (35g) icing sugar in a bowl, stirring until the sugar dissolves. Set aside.

Divide the sponge cake among six 1 1/2 cup (375ml) serving dishes, drizzle with the Cointreau mixture, then scatter over half the Turkish delight. Stir the rosewater into the custard, then pour into the serving dishes.

Whip the cream and remaining icing sugar together until soft peaks form, then fold through the yoghurt. Dollop over the custard and chill for at least 6 hours.

If desired, drizzle the trifles with pomegranate juice and garnish with pomegranate seeds, rose petals and pistachios. Serve trifles topped with the remaining Turkish delight. **Serves 6**

* Rosewater and dried rose petals are from Middle Eastern food shops. Pomegranates are available in season from greengrocers and selected supermarkets.

LEMON MERINGUE
BREAD & BUTTER PUDDING

50g unsalted butter, softened
1 cup (325g) good-quality
    lemon curd*
10 white bread slices,
    crusts removed
1^1/2 cups (375ml) milk
^{1}/2 cup (125ml) pure (thin)
    cream, plus extra to serve
Finely grated zest of 1 lemon
4 eggs, separated,
    plus extra 1 eggwhite
185g caster sugar

Spread the butter and lemon curd on one side of each bread slice. Cut in half on the diagonal to make 20 triangles, then arrange in a greased 1 litre baking dish, overlapping slightly and forming 2 layers.

Place the milk, cream and zest in a saucepan over medium heat and bring to just below boiling point. Remove from heat and stand for 10 minutes to infuse.

Preheat the oven to 170°C.

Place the egg yolks and ^{1}/2 cup (110g) sugar in a bowl and beat with electric beaters until thick and pale. Slowly pour in the milk mixture, beating to combine. Strain, then pour over the bread. Stand for 15 minutes to allow the custard to soak in.

Bake the pudding for 30 minutes or until just set.

Meanwhile, place all the eggwhites in a clean, dry bowl and whisk with electric beaters until soft peaks form. Gradually add the remaining ^{1}/3 cup (75g) sugar, whisking constantly, until glossy and stiff peaks form.

Increase the oven temperature to 200°C.

Spread the meringue over the top of the pudding using the back of a spoon, then return to the oven and bake for 6-8 minutes until meringue is tinged golden. Serve warm with extra cream. **Serves 6**

* Available from delis and gourmet food shops.

WINTER MENUS

Orient express

STARTER
Singapore noodles

MAIN
Thai beef curry
with holy basil

DESSERT
Coconut creme
caramel

136

156

170

132

154

168

Family favourites

STARTER
Curried carrot
& lentil soup

MAIN
Pork & fennel tray bake
with Moroccan spice

DESSERT
Sticky date tart
with toffee sauce

A touch of spice

STARTER
Potato 'tacos'
with tomato salsa

MAIN
Chorizo-crusted
blue-eye with beans

DESSERT
Poached pears
with sweet labne

138

158

178

144

162

180

Exotic feast

STARTER
Crispy polenta with
truffled mushrooms
and Taleggio

MAIN
Lamb & kumara tagine

DESSERT
Persian trifle

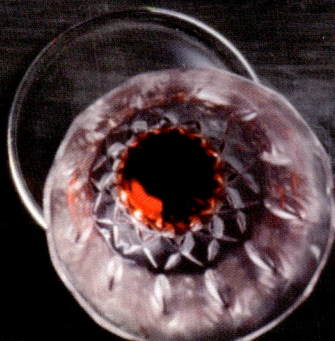

in season

artichokes asparagus beans (broad, flat, snake)

broccolini cabbage cherries leeks papaya

passionfruit peas pineapple radishes snow peas

strawberries watercress watermelon

SPRING

GOAT'S CHEESE TRUFFLES

These colourful nibbles are best enjoyed with a glass of wine. Use a variety of coatings, including spices, seeds and chopped herbs, to create different flavours and textures.

1½ cups (300g) soft
  goat's cheese
2 tbs honey

**Toppings (enough to
coat 3 balls of each)**
2 tbs sesame seeds, toasted
2 tbs sweet paprika
2 tbs chopped flat-leaf
  parsley leaves
2 tbs sumac*
2 tbs zaatar (Middle Eastern
  spice blend)*
2 tbs shichimi togarashi
  (Japanese spice mix)*
2 tbs poppyseeds

Place the goat's cheese in a bowl, season, then roll into 21 balls, using about 2 heaped teaspoons of cheese for each. Chill for 30 minutes to firm up.

Combine honey with a few drops of warm water, then brush over the balls.

Place each topping on a separate plate, then roll the goat's cheese in the toppings to coat well. Keep chilled until ready to serve. **Makes 21**

* Sumac (a lemony Middle Eastern spice) and zaatar are from delis and Middle Eastern food shops. Shichimi togarashi is from Asian food shops.

WASABI PANCAKES WITH SMOKED OCEAN TROUT

These small pancakes are great to serve as canapés with aperitifs, or you could turn them into larger pancakes for a sit-down starter.

125g self-raising flour
1/4 tsp baking powder
1 egg
1 tsp Dijon mustard
2/3 cup (185ml) milk
1 tsp wasabi paste*
1 tbs chopped dill, plus
    extra dill sprigs to serve
Sunflower oil, to brush
200g sliced smoked
    ocean trout
60g salmon roe*

Wasabi creme fraiche
200g creme fraiche
1 tbs chopped flat-leaf
    parsley leaves
1 tbs chopped dill
1 tsp wasabi paste*

Place the flour, baking powder, egg, mustard, milk, wasabi paste and dill in a food processor, season, then whiz to combine. Pour into a jug and stand at room temperature for 30 minutes.

Meanwhile, for the wasabi creme fraiche, combine all the ingredients together in a bowl and season. Keep chilled until ready to serve.

Brush a non-stick frypan with a little oil and place over medium heat. In batches, drop 2 teaspoons pancake batter into the frypan for each pancake (or use 2 tablespoons for larger pancakes). Cook for 1-2 minutes each side until golden. Keep warm while you cook the remaining pancakes.

Stack the pancakes on serving plates. Top with wasabi creme fraiche, ocean trout slices and a few pearls of salmon roe. Serve garnished with dill sprigs.
Makes 36 small pancakes or 10 large pancakes

* Wasabi paste is from selected supermarkets and Asian food shops. Salmon roe is from delis, gourmet food shops and fishmongers.

BROWN RICE & LENTIL SALAD

My inspiration for this comes from Matt Wilkinson, one of my favourite Australian chefs. He served a similar dish as part of a grazing menu when I visited his cafe, Pope Joan, in Melbourne.

2 cups (400g) brown rice
1/4 cup (60ml) extra virgin
    olive oil
2 red onions, thinly sliced
1/4 cup (60ml) red wine vinegar
400g can lentils, rinsed,
    drained
1/2 cup (80g) sultanas
Juice of 1 lemon
1 long red chilli, seeds
    removed, chopped
1/2 cup flat-leaf parsley
    leaves, chopped
1/4 cup (40g) sunflower seeds
200g marinated feta, drained,
    crumbled
1/3 cup mint leaves, chopped,
    plus extra leaves to serve
Tomato kasundi* or
    good-quality tomato
    chutney, to serve

Cook the rice according to the packet instructions. Rinse under cold water, drain, then set aside.

Meanwhile, place 1 tablespoon oil in a frypan over medium heat. Add the onion and a pinch of salt, then cook, stirring, for 6-8 minutes until soft and caramelised. Add the vinegar and cook, stirring, for 2 minutes, then set aside to cool.

Place the rice and onion in a serving bowl with the remaining ingredients, except for the kasundi, and toss well to combine. Top salad with extra mint leaves and serve with the tomato kasundi or chutney.
Serves 4 (or 6 as a side)

* Available from delis and gourmet food shops.

BAKED RICOTTA & ZUCCHINI SLICE

This slice is wonderful for brunch. You can even make it the night before and keep it in the fridge, then gently warm in the oven before serving.

3 pontiac or desiree potatoes
   (about 600g), peeled
1½ tbs olive oil
6 bacon rashers,
   finely chopped
2 zucchinis
2 eggs, lightly beaten
1kg fresh ricotta, well drained
¼ cup (20g) finely
   grated parmesan
500g vine-ripened
   cherry tomatoes
Small basil leaves and pesto
   (see Extras, p 246), to serve

Preheat the oven to 180°C and grease a 25cm x 10cm loaf pan or terrine.

Place the potatoes in a saucepan of cold, salted water. Bring to a boil over medium-high heat, then cook for 8 minutes to par-boil. Drain, cool, then coarsely grate into a large bowl.

Meanwhile, place 2 teaspoons oil in a frypan over medium-high heat. Add the bacon and cook, stirring, for 2-3 minutes until crisp. Drain on paper towel, then add to the grated potato.

Coarsely grate the zucchinis, then enclose in a muslin cloth or clean Chux and squeeze to remove excess liquid. Add the zucchini to the potato mixture with the eggs, ricotta and parmesan, then stir well to combine. Season well.

Spread the ricotta mixture into the loaf pan. Bake for 25-30 minutes until puffed and golden. Cool for 10 minutes in the pan.

Increase the oven to 220°C.

Place the tomatoes in a roasting pan, drizzle with the remaining 1 tablespoon oil and season. Roast for 10 minutes or until softened and starting to collapse.

Turn out the baked ricotta onto a chopping board and cut into 2cm-thick slices. Serve warm or at room temperature with roasted tomatoes, basil leaves and a dollop of pesto. **Serves 6-8**

SPINACH GNUDI WITH SAGE BURNT BUTTER

Gnudi is a type of gnocchi made with ricotta, resulting in fluffy dumplings that are much lighter than the potato version. All they need is a simple sage butter sauce.

150g English spinach,
   stems removed
1½ cups (360g) fresh ricotta,
   well drained
Pinch of ground nutmeg
¾ cup (60g) finely grated
   parmesan, plus extra
   to serve
2 egg yolks, lightly beaten
½ cup (75g) plain flour, sifted,
   plus extra to dust
100g unsalted butter
16 sage leaves

Cook the spinach leaves in saucepan of boiling, salted water for 1 minute or until just wilted. Drain and refresh under cold water, then squeeze out as much liquid as possible.

Finely chop the spinach, then place in a bowl with the ricotta, nutmeg, parmesan and egg. Season and stir to combine, then mix in the flour. The mixture should be slightly sticky, but not too wet – add a little more flour if needed. Shape the ricotta mixture into walnut-sized balls, then lightly dust with flour.

In batches, cook the gnudi in a large saucepan of salted, simmering water for 1-2 minutes until they rise to the surface. Remove with a slotted spoon and set aside on a plate.

Meanwhile, melt the butter in a frypan over medium heat. Add the sage and cook for 2-3 minutes until the sage is crisp and the butter is just starting to brown.

Add the gnudi to the frypan and gently toss to combine. Divide gnudi and sage burnt butter among plates and serve sprinkled with extra parmesan.

Serves 4

SUSHI STACKS

125g short-grain sushi rice*
1¹/₂ tbs rice vinegar
1 tsp caster sugar
1 tsp wasabi paste*,
  plus extra to serve
1¹/₂ tsp finely grated ginger
1 tbs lime juice
350g sashimi-grade salmon,
  pin-boned, cut into
  1cm pieces
1 Lebanese cucumber,
  seeds removed, chopped
Black sesame seeds*, chopped
  chives, micro herbs or
  coriander and soy sauce,
  to serve

Rinse the rice under cold water until the water runs clear. Place the rice in a saucepan with 200ml cold water. Cover with a lid, bring to the boil, then reduce the heat to low and cook for 10 minutes. Remove from the heat and stand, covered, for 10 minutes or until the water is absorbed – don't be tempted to lift the lid early as you will loose the steam that cooks the rice. Combine the vinegar, sugar and ¹/₂ teaspoon salt in a small bowl, then stir into the rice. Allow to cool.

Stir the wasabi paste, ginger and lime juice together in a bowl. Add the salmon and cucumber, then toss gently to combine.

Place a 7cm x 3cm ring mould on each serving plate, then divide the rice mixture among the moulds. (Alternatively, place small mounds of rice on each plate.) Top with the salmon mixture, then remove the moulds, if using. Scatter with sesame seeds and herbs, then serve immediately with soy sauce and extra wasabi. **Serves 6**

* Sushi rice, wasabi paste and black sesame seeds are from selected supermarkets and Asian food shops. Sashimi-grade salmon is from fishmongers.

ASPARAGUS & RICOTTA TART

1 quantity shortcrust pastry
   (see Extras, p 246) or
   445g packet Careme Sour
   Cream Shortcrust Pastry*
1 egg
250g fresh ricotta, well drained
1/4 cup (60ml) pure (thin) cream
1/4 cup (60ml) milk
1/4 cup basil leaves
2 tbs chopped chives
2 bunches asparagus,
   woody ends trimmed
Micro herbs or extra basil,
   to serve

Preheat the oven to 200°C and grease a 30cm x 20cm rectangular loose-bottomed tart pan.

Roll out the pastry to 5mm thick if using homemade. Use the pastry to line the tart pan, trimming the excess. Chill for 10 minutes.

Line the pastry with baking paper and fill with pastry weights or uncooked rice. Bake for 10 minutes, then remove the paper and weights. Bake for a further 3 minutes or until golden and dry. Cool slightly.

Reduce the oven to 180°C.

Place the egg, ricotta, cream, milk, basil and chives in a food processor, season, then whiz to combine. Spread the ricotta mixture into the tart shell, then arrange the asparagus spears on top.

Bake for 25 minutes or until the filling is set. Cool slightly, then cut the tart into slices and serve scattered with herbs. **Serves 4-6**

* From delis and gourmet food shops; for stockists, visit: caremepastry.com.

BURRATA WITH PROSCIUTTO AND PEAS

Burrata is an Italian cheese that has an outer layer of mozzarella and a soft creamy centre of unspun curds. It's available from good Italian delis and specialist cheese shops, but if you can't find it, use buffalo mozzarella instead.

1½ cups fresh or frozen peas
¹/₃ cup (80ml) extra virgin
   olive oil
2 tbs lemon juice, plus
   lemon wedges to serve
1 cup (80g) finely
   grated parmesan
2 x 200g burrata balls,
   roughly torn
8 thin prosciutto slices
¹/₃ cup small mint leaves
Chargrilled sourdough,
   to serve

Cook the fresh peas in a saucepan of boiling, salted water for 5-6 minutes (or 2-3 minutes for frozen) until tender. Drain, then refresh under cold water. Place in a bowl and roughly mash with a fork.

Whisk the olive oil and lemon juice together and season. Toss half the dressing with the peas, then stir through half the parmesan.

Divide half the peas among serving plates and top with burrata and prosciutto. Top with the remaining peas and drizzle with remaining dressing. Scatter with mint leaves and remaining parmesan. Season, then serve with chargrilled sourdough and lemon wedges.
Serves 4

BULGOGI WITH EASY PICKLE

I love going out for Korean barbecue. It's always great fun cooking the different meats on the grill in the centre of the table, especially my favourite dish – bulgogi. The best part is, it's easy to replicate the experience at home.

300g beef fillet steak
100ml soy sauce
1 small onion, grated
1 tsp sesame oil
2 tsp finely grated ginger
2 tbs brown sugar
3 garlic cloves, finely chopped
2 butter lettuces,
    leaves separated
Steamed jasmine rice,
    shredded spring onion and
    thinly sliced chillies, to serve

Pickled vegetables

90g caster sugar
$^2/_3$ cup (185ml) rice vinegar
1 carrot, cut into thin
    matchsticks
$^1/_2$ daikon*, peeled, cut
    into thin matchsticks

Enclose the beef in plastic wrap, then freeze for 1 hour (this will make it easier to slice).

Combine the soy sauce, onion, sesame oil, ginger, brown sugar and garlic in a bowl. Using a sharp knife, very thinly slice the beef, then add to the marinade. Cover and chill for at least 2 hours.

Meanwhile, for the pickled vegetables, place the caster sugar, vinegar, 100ml water and a good pinch of salt in a saucepan over medium-low heat, stirring until the sugar dissolves. Remove from the heat, then add the vegetables and stand for 2 hours to pickle.

Preheat a barbecue or chargrill pan over high heat.

Drain the beef, discarding the marinade. In batches if necessary, cook the beef for 10 seconds each side or until charred.

Divide the lettuce among plates and top with the rice, beef, spring onion and chilli. Drain the pickled vegetables and serve with the bulgogi. **Serves 4-6**

* From greengrocers and Asian food shops.

SPAGHETTI WITH PEAS, LEMON AND CHILLI

400g spaghetti or
 other long pasta
1$\frac{1}{2}$ cups fresh or frozen peas
3 long red chillies, seeds
 removed, finely chopped
300ml thickened cream
2 cups basil leaves, torn
1 cup mint leaves, torn
1 bunch chives, chopped
Finely grated zest
 and juice of 1 lemon
$\frac{2}{3}$ cup (100g) pine nuts,
 toasted
Finely grated parmesan
 and extra virgin olive oil,
 to serve

Cook the pasta in a saucepan of boiling, salted water according to the packet instructions, adding the fresh peas for the final 5 minutes of cooking time (or 3 minutes for frozen). Drain.

Return the pasta and peas to the warm saucepan. Add the chilli, cream, herbs, lemon zest and nuts, then toss gently together until just combined. Add the lemon juice to taste, then season.

Divide the pasta among plates. Sprinkle with the parmesan and serve drizzled with olive oil. **Serves 4**

MINUTE STEAKS WITH PAN-FRIED POTATOES

This makes a great midweek dinner. I like to keep different herb butters in my freezer to add an instant flavour hit to grilled meats and fish.

1 garlic clove, finely chopped
2 tbs chopped oregano leaves
2 tbs olive oil
4 x 120g minute steaks
Herb butter (see Extras, p 246)
 and green beans, to serve

Pan-fried potatoes
4 potatoes (such as pontiac
 or King Edward), peeled,
 cut into 2cm cubes
2 tbs olive oil

For the pan-fried potatoes, place the potato in a saucepan of cold, salted water. Bring to the boil over medium-high heat and cook for 3 minutes to par-boil. Drain and return to the warm pan, then cover with a lid and shake the saucepan to fluff up the surface of the potato. Place oil in a frypan over medium-high heat. Once hot, add the potato to the frypan, season, then cook, turning, for 8-10 minutes until crisp and golden.

Meanwhile, combine the garlic, oregano and oil in a small bowl and season, then brush over the steaks.

Place a chargrill pan or frypan over high heat. Once the pan is hot, cook the steaks, in 2 batches, for 30 seconds each side or until just cooked.

Divide the steaks among plates, drizzle with any pan juices and top with some herb butter. Serve with pan-fried potatoes and green beans. **Serves 4**

SPRING SAUSAGE BAKE

We love sausages in my house, especially now that you can buy such good-quality varieties from your local butcher. This recipe is a great way to liven them up by simply adding some vegies and a good dollop of pesto.

2 fennel bulbs, trimmed,
    cut into wedges
1 red onion, cut into wedges
2 zucchinis, thickly sliced
1 whole garlic bulb,
    halved horizontally
2 bay leaves
12 good-quality pork
    chipolata sausages
1/3 cup (80ml) olive oil
2 tbs balsamic vinegar
1 tsp chopped thyme leaves
1 tsp chopped rosemary leaves
400g mixed small heirloom
    tomatoes* or vine-ripened
    cherry tomatoes, halved
    if large
Pesto (see Extras, p 246)
    and basil leaves, to serve

Preheat the oven to 200°C.

Place the fennel, onion, zucchini, garlic, bay leaves and sausages in a roasting pan. Drizzle with the olive oil and balsamic vinegar, scatter with the thyme and rosemary, then season.

Bake for 20 minutes, turning once, or until the vegetables are tender. Add the tomatoes to the pan and return to the oven for a further 3-4 minutes until the tomatoes have started to soften and the sausages are cooked through.

Dollop the sausage bake with the pesto and serve scattered with basil leaves. **Serves 4**

* From greengrocers and selected supermarkets.

SALMON WITH SPICED CARROT SAUCE

Lately, I've been trying to find another use for my juicer other than making my morning blend. So far, I've had great success adding fresh juices to risottos, soups and even this Asian-inspired sauce. If you don't have a juicer, pick some up from your local juice bar.

350ml fresh carrot juice
1 tbs Thai red curry paste
2cm piece ginger,
   peeled, sliced
1 lemongrass stalk
   (inner core only), bruised
2 kaffir lime leaves*,
   plus extra shredded
   kaffir lime leaves to serve
1 garlic clove, bruised
Finely grated zest
   and juice of 1 orange
1 tsp caster sugar
Juice of 1 lime
1/2 cup (125ml) coconut milk
2 tbs sunflower oil
4 x 180g skinless salmon
   fillets, pin-boned, cut into
   3cm pieces
Steamed rice, thinly sliced red
   chilli and micro coriander or
   coriander leaves, to serve

Place the carrot juice, curry paste, ginger, lemongrass, kaffir lime leaves, garlic and orange zest in a saucepan over medium heat. Bring to a simmer, then cook for 3 minutes. Cover, then remove from the heat and stand for 20 minutes to infuse.

Return the saucepan to medium heat. Add the sugar and orange and lime juices, stirring until the sugar dissolves. Strain into a clean saucepan, discarding the solids, then season and stir in the coconut milk. Gently warm over low heat.

Meanwhile, place the sunflower oil in a frypan over medium-high heat. Season the salmon, then cook, turning, for 4 minutes or until almost cooked through, but still a little rare in the centre.

Divide the steamed rice among deep bowls. Top with the salmon and ladle over the spiced carrot sauce. Serve garnished with chilli, coriander and shredded kaffir lime leaves. **Serves 4**

* Available from greengrocers.

SUMAC LAMB CUTLETS WITH FATTOUSH

1 tbs sumac*
Juice of 1 lemon
1/2 cup (125ml) olive oil
2 garlic cloves, finely chopped
12 French-trimmed
    lamb cutlets
2 tsp Dijon mustard
2 tbs finely chopped
    mint leaves

Fattoush

12 cherry tomatoes, halved
1 round Lebanese bread,
    toasted, broken into pieces
100g marinated feta, drained
1 baby cos, leaves torn
1 cup mint leaves,
    plus extra to serve
1 cup flat-leaf parsley leaves
1 cup coriander leaves,
    plus extra to serve
1 cup mixed olives
1 Lebanese cucumber,
    chopped

Place the sumac, 1 tablespoon lemon juice, 1/4 cup (60ml) oil and half the garlic in a glass or ceramic dish and season. Add the lamb cutlets, turning to coat in the marinade, then set aside for 30 minutes.

Meanwhile, place the mustard and remaining lemon juice and garlic in a bowl, then whisk to combine. Add the remaining oil in a slow, steady stream, whisking constantly, until you have a thick dressing. Season, then stir through the mint. Set aside.

For the fattoush, place all the ingredients in a large serving bowl and toss to combine. Set aside.

Preheat a barbecue or chargrill pan over high heat.

In batches if necessary, cook the lamb cutlets for 2-3 minutes each side for medium-rare or until cooked to your liking.

Toss the fattoush with half the dressing. Garnish the lamb cutlets with extra mint and coriander leaves, then serve with the fattoush and remaining dressing.
Serves 4-6

* Sumac is a lemony Middle Eastern spice available from delis and selected supermarkets.

214

VITELLO TONNATO BURGERS

Vitello tonnato (veal with a tuna and mayonnaise sauce) is one of my all-time favourite Italian dishes, but sadly not one of my sons'. So I transformed it into a burger and now it's a much-loved family special.

800g veal mince
1 small onion, finely chopped
1 garlic clove, finely chopped
¼ cup (65g) capers in brine,
    rinsed, drained, chopped,
    plus 2 tbs whole capers
¼ cup (40g) chopped
    black olives
Finely grated zest of 1 lemon
¼ cup finely chopped
    flat-leaf parsley leaves
1 tbs olive oil,
    plus extra to brush
4 burger buns, split, toasted
Salad leaves, sliced tomatoes
    and lemon wedges, to serve

Tonnato sauce

185g can tuna in oil, drained
1 cup (300g) whole-egg
    mayonnaise
1 tbs capers, rinsed, drained
2 tsp grated lemon zest,
    plus 1 tbs lemon juice
1-2 anchovy fillets in oil
    (optional), drained

Place the veal mince, onion, garlic, chopped capers, olives, lemon zest and parsley in a bowl. Season, then mix well to combine. Shape into four thick burger patties and chill for 1 hour to firm up.

Meanwhile, heat the olive oil in a frypan over medium-high heat. Cook the whole capers for 1 minute or until crisp. Set aside.

For the tonnato sauce, place all the ingredients in a blender and whiz to a smooth sauce. Set aside.

Preheat a barbecue or chargrill pan over high heat.

Brush the burger patties with a little oil and grill for 2-3 minutes each side until cooked through.

Spread some tonnato sauce on the bun bases, then top with the salad leaves, burger patties, more tonnato sauce, fried capers and tomato. Sandwich with the bun tops and serve with lemon wedges.

Serves 4

LAMB & HARISSA PIZZA WITH TABOULI AND YOGHURT

2 tbs extra virgin olive oil,
  plus extra to serve
1 onion, finely chopped
1 garlic clove, finely chopped
500g lamb mince
2 tsp ground cumin
1/2 tsp ground cinnamon
1 cup (250ml) beef stock
1 tbs harissa (North African
  chilli paste)*
2 tbs chopped flat-leaf
  parsley leaves
2 tbs chopped mint leaves
2 plain pizza bases
1 cup (260g) hummus
Thick Greek-style yoghurt,
  to serve

Tabouli
2 tbs burghul (cracked wheat)*
1/2 bunch flat-leaf parsley,
  leaves finely chopped
1 bunch mint, leaves finely
  chopped, plus extra to serve
2 tomatoes, seeds removed,
  finely chopped
2 red onions, finely chopped
1 tbs lemon juice

Preheat the oven to 200°C.

For the tabouli, soak the burghul in boiling water for 15 minutes, then drain. Toss the burghul with the remaining tabouli ingredients and season. Set aside.

Meanwhile, place the olive oil in a frypan over medium heat. Add the onion and cook, stirring, for 2-3 minutes until softened. Add the garlic and lamb, then cook, breaking up any lumps with a wooden spoon, for 4-5 minutes until the lamb is browned. Add the cumin, cinnamon, stock and 2 teaspoons harissa, then cook, stirring, for 1-2 minutes until the liquid has evaporated. Stir in the parsley and mint, then season.

Place each pizza base on a baking tray or pizza stone. Combine the hummus and remaining 2 teaspoons harissa, then spread over the pizza bases. Scatter with the lamb mixture, then bake for 5 minutes or until the edges are starting to crisp.

Scatter tabouli over the pizzas and top with dollops of yoghurt. Drizzle with extra olive oil, then serve garnished with extra mint. **Serves 4**

* Harissa is available from delis and gourmet food shops. Burghul is available from health food shops and selected supermarkets.

PRAWN PILAU

1 cup (200g) basmati rice
1 tsp ground turmeric
$^1/_4$ cup (60ml) sunflower oil
1 onion, finely chopped
1 cinnamon quill
5 cloves
6 cardamom pods, bruised
10 fresh curry leaves*
1 lemongrass stalk (inner core
   only), finely chopped
4 garlic cloves,
   finely chopped
5cm piece ginger,
   finely grated
600g peeled green prawns
30g unsalted butter
1 tbs chopped
   coriander leaves
1 tbs chopped dill
Lemon wedges and
   mango chutney, to serve

Place the rice and $^1/_2$ teaspoon turmeric in a saucepan of cold, salted water. Bring to a simmer over medium heat. Cook for 5 minutes, then drain and set aside.

Meanwhile, place the oil in a deep frypan (with a lid) over medium-low heat. Add the onion, cinnamon, cloves, cardamom, curry leaves and lemongrass, then cook, stirring, for 5-6 minutes until onion has softened. Stir in the garlic, ginger and remaining $^1/_2$ teaspoon turmeric, then add the prawns and cook, stirring, for 2-3 minutes until just cooked. Add the rice, stirring to coat the grains, then add $^1/_2$ cup (125ml) water and 1 teaspoon salt. Cover with a lid and cook for 5 minutes. Remove from heat and stand, covered, for 5 minutes or until all the liquid has been absorbed – don't be tempted to lift the lid early as you will loose the steam that cooks the rice.

Add the butter to the pilau and fluff up with a fork. Stir in the herbs and serve with lemon wedges and mango chutney. **Serves 4**

* From greengrocers and selected supermarkets.

CRISPY FISH BURRITOS WITH SALSA CRIOLLA

Salsa criolla is an Argentinian salsa traditionally served with *asado* (barbecued) meats, but it also makes a wonderful accompaniment to these fish burritos.

1²/₃ cups (250g)
   self-raising flour
Pinch of dried chilli flakes
1 egg, lightly beaten
375ml chilled lager
Sunflower oil, to deep-fry
4 x 180g flathead fillets,
   halved lengthways
8 flour tortillas
Sour cream, thinly sliced
   avocado and lime wedges,
   to serve

Salsa criolla

2 vine-ripened tomatoes, seeds
   removed, finely chopped
1 small red onion,
   finely chopped
1 garlic clove, crushed
1 long red chilli, seeds
   removed, finely chopped
¼ cup (60ml) red wine vinegar
1 tbs caster sugar
¼ cup chopped coriander
   leaves, plus extra sprigs
   to serve
2 tbs olive oil

Place the flour, chilli flakes and 1 teaspoon sea salt in a bowl. Add the egg, then gradually whisk in the lager until just combined. Cover and chill for 30 minutes.

Meanwhile, for the salsa criolla, place all the ingredients in a bowl, season, then stir well to combine. Set aside.

Preheat the oven to 150°C.

Half-fill a large saucepan or deep fryer with oil and heat to 190°C (if you don't have a kitchen thermometer, a cube of bread dropped into the oil will turn golden after 30 seconds when the oil is hot enough). Pat fish dry with paper towel, then season. In batches, dip the fish into the beer batter, shaking off excess, then deep-fry for 3-4 minutes until crisp and golden. Remove with a slotted spoon and drain on paper towel. Transfer to a baking tray and keep warm in the oven while you cook the remaining fish.

Enclose the tortillas in foil and warm in the oven as you cook the final batch of fish.

Spread the tortillas with a little sour cream, then top with avocado, fish, some salsa criolla and coriander sprigs. Season, then roll up and serve with lime wedges and remaining salsa. **Serves 4**

THAI CHICKEN & PUMPKIN CAKES

600g Jap or butternut
    pumpkin, peeled, chopped
1/3 cup (80ml) sunflower oil
1 bunch coriander
500g chicken mince
1 cup (70g) fresh breadcrumbs
3 kaffir lime leaves*,
    finely shredded
1 lemongrass stalk (inner core
    only), finely chopped
1 tbs Thai red curry paste
1 tbs fish sauce
2 garlic cloves, finely chopped
2 tsp sesame oil
Salad leaves, steamed rice,
    lime wedges and sweet
    chilli sauce, to serve

Preheat the oven to 180°C and line a baking tray with baking paper.

Place the pumpkin on the baking tray, drizzle with 1 tablespoon sunflower oil and season. Cover with foil, then bake for 25 minutes or until tender. Transfer to a large bowl, then mash with a potato masher or a fork until smooth. Allow to cool.

Finely chop the coriander roots, stems and leaves, then add to the cooled pumpkin with the chicken mince, breadcrumbs, kaffir lime leaves, lemongrass, curry paste, fish sauce and garlic. Mix well to combine, season, then shape into 12 thick patties. Chill for 15 minutes to firm up.

Place the sesame oil and remaining 1/4 cup (60ml) sunflower oil in a frypan over medium-high heat. Cook the cakes for 1-2 minutes each side until browned, then place on a baking paper-lined baking tray and bake for 10 minutes or until cooked through.

Serve the chicken and pumpkin cakes with salad, rice, lime wedges and sweet chilli sauce. **Serves 4**

* Available from greengrocers and Asian food shops.

CHERRY CLAFOUTIS

½ cup (75g) plain flour
600ml pure (thin) cream,
  plus extra whipped cream
  to serve
5 eggs, plus extra 7 egg yolks
1½ cups (330g) caster sugar
670g jar morello cherries
  in syrup, drained,
  syrup reserved
1 vanilla bean, split,
  seeds scraped

Whisk the flour, cream, eggs, extra egg yolks and 1 cup (220g) sugar together until smooth. Stand the batter at room temperature for 1 hour.

Meanwhile, place the reserved cherry syrup, vanilla pod and seeds, and remaining ½ cup (110g) sugar in a saucepan over low heat, stirring until the sugar dissolves. Increase the heat to medium and simmer for 5 minutes or until reduced and syrupy. Allow to cool, then remove the vanilla pod.

Preheat the oven to 160°C and grease a 2 litre baking dish.

Place the drained cherries in the baking dish, then pour over the batter. Bake for 1 hour or until puffed and golden. Cool in the dish for 10 minutes.

Cut the clafoutis into squares and serve warm with whipped cream and the vanilla and cherry syrup.
Serves 6-8

LAVENDER & RICOTTA MOUSSE

The scent of lavender reminds me of Provence. This cheat's mousse encapsulates the essence of the French region and provides the perfect end to a perfect spring lunch.

500g fresh ricotta, well drained
1/4 cup (55g) caster sugar
1/2 cup (125ml) pure
   (thin) cream
1 cup (100g) finely grated
   white chocolate
1 tsp vanilla extract
2/3 cup (100g) chopped
   pistachio kernels
1 tsp dried lavender*

Orange syrup
Thinly zested rind of 1 lemon
Thinly zested rind of
   2 oranges, plus 1/2 cup
   (125ml) orange juice
1/2 cup (110g) caster sugar
1 tbs Grand Marnier or other
   orange liqueur (optional)

For the orange syrup, place the lemon and orange rind in a saucepan and cover with cold water. Simmer over medium heat for 10 minutes, then drain. Repeat this blanching method 2 more times. (This will remove the bitterness from the rind.) Place sugar and 1/2 cup (125ml) water in a saucepan over low heat, stirring until sugar dissolves. Add the blanched rind and simmer for 5 minutes or until the rind is almost translucent. Strain into a clean saucepan, reserving the rind. Place over low heat, then add orange juice and cook for 3-4 minutes until reduced and syrupy. Stir in the liqueur, if using, and the reserved rind, then allow to cool completely. Set aside.

Combine the drained ricotta and sugar in a bowl. Stir in the cream, white chocolate, vanilla, pistachios and lavender until just combined.

Place a 7cm x 3cm ring mould on each serving plate, then divide the ricotta mixture among the moulds. (Alternatively, just scoop onto plates.) Remove the ring moulds, if using, then serve with orange syrup. **Serves 6**

* Available from gourmet food shops.

ROSE & RASPBERRY MERINGUE TARTS

1 quantity sweet shortcrust
  pastry (see Extras, p 246)
  or 435g packet Careme
  Vanilla Bean Sweet
  Shortcrust Pastry*
500g fresh or frozen,
  thawed raspberries,
  plus extra to serve
2 tsp rosewater*
$1/3$ cup (50g) arrowroot
2 tbs lemon juice
260g caster sugar
4 eggs, separated
50g unsalted butter

Grease six 10cm loose-bottomed tart pans.

Roll out the pastry to 5mm thick if using homemade. Use the pastry to line the tart pans, trimming the excess. Chill while you make the filling.

Puree the raspberries in a blender, then pass through a sieve into a saucepan, pressing down with the back of a spoon to extract as much juice as possible and discarding the solids. Stir in the rosewater.

Place the arrowroot and $1/3$ cup (80ml) cold water in a bowl, stirring to combine, then add to the saucepan with the lemon juice and $1/2$ cup (110g) sugar. Place over low heat and cook, stirring, for 3-4 minutes until thick. Add the egg yolks, 1 at a time, beating well with a wooden spoon after each addition. Add the butter and stir until melted. Remove from the heat and allow to cool, then chill for 30 minutes.

Preheat the oven to 180°C.

Line the tart shells with baking paper and pastry weights or uncooked rice, then bake for 10 minutes. Remove the paper and weights, then bake for a further 5 minutes or until golden and dry. Cool, then fill the tart shells with the chilled raspberry mixture.

Beat the eggwhites with electric beaters until soft peaks form. Gradually add remaining $2/3$ cup (150g) sugar, beating until stiff peaks form, then pipe or spoon over the filling. Brown meringue with a kitchen blowtorch or bake in a 200°C oven for 2-3 minutes until tinged golden. Serve with extra berries. **Serves 6**

* From delis and gourmet food shops; for Careme stockists, visit: caremepastry.com.

PINEAPPLE CARPACCIO WITH SOUR CREAM ICE CREAM

This pineapple carpaccio is the ideal refresher after a spicy meal. If you don't want to make your own ice cream, a good-quality coconut or vanilla ice cream works just as well.

2 tbs white sugar
1 cup mint leaves, plus
    extra leaves to serve
1/2 vanilla bean, split,
    seeds scraped
1 small or 1/2 large pineapple,
    peeled, cored
Edible flowers* (optional),
    to serve

Sour cream ice cream

2 1/2 cups (600g) sour cream
1 cup (220g) caster sugar
1 tbs glucose syrup*
Finely grated zest and
    juice of 1 small lemon

For the sour cream ice cream, place all the ingredients in a bowl and beat together with a wooden spoon. Stand for 20 minutes to allow the flavours to develop, then transfer to an ice cream machine and churn according to the manufacturer's instructions. (Alternatively, pour the mixture into a shallow container and freeze for 2 hours or until frozen at the edges. Remove from the freezer and beat with electric beaters, then return to the freezer. Repeat the process 2-3 times.) Freeze for 4 hours or until firm.

Place the white sugar, mint leaves and vanilla seeds in a mortar and pestle, then pound until the mint has broken up. Set mint and vanilla sugar aside.

Cut the pineapple lengthways into wedges, then very thinly slice (a mandoline is ideal).

Arrange the pineapple on plates, then serve with the sour cream ice cream, mint and vanilla sugar, extra mint leaves and edible flowers, if desired. **Serves 6-8**

* Edible flowers are available from farmers' markets and selected greengrocers. Glucose syrup is available from the baking aisle in supermarkets.

CHOCOLATE CHEESECAKE WITH COCOA NIB CREAM

2 x 150g packets Oreo biscuits
    or other cream-filled
    chocolate biscuits
125g unsalted butter,
    melted, cooled
250g cream cheese,
    at room temperature
2 cups (500g) mascarpone
1/3 cup (75g) caster sugar
3 eggs
1/2 cup (50g) cocoa powder
100g dark chocolate,
    melted, cooled
1 tbs chocolate liqueur
    (optional)
1 cup (120g) cocoa nibs
    (roast cocoa bean pieces)*,
    plus extra to serve
300ml thickened cream,
    lightly whipped

Grease and line a 24cm springform cake pan with baking paper.

Place the biscuits in a food processor and whiz to fine crumbs. Add the butter and pulse a few times to combine, then press into the base the cake pan. Chill for 30 minutes to firm up.

Preheat the oven to 170°C.

Place the cream cheese, mascarpone and caster sugar in the cleaned food processor and whiz to combine. Add the eggs and whiz to combine, then add the cocoa, chocolate and liqueur, if using, and whiz until very smooth. Add half the cocoa nibs and pulse to combine, then spread the mascarpone mixture over the biscuit base.

Bake for 45-50 minutes until the cake is firm to the touch, but still has a slight wobble. Turn off the oven and allow the cheesecake to cool completely in the oven with the door slightly ajar. Once cooled, chill for 2-3 hours until firm.

Fold the remaining 1/2 cup (60g) cocoa nibs into the whipped cream. Top the cheesecake with the cocoa nib cream and serve sprinkled with extra cocoa nibs.

Serves 8

* Available from gourmet food shops and specialist chocolate shops.

CHILLED RICE PUDDING WITH BLUEBERRY COMPOTE

1/3 cup (75g) arborio rice
or other short-grain rice
2 cups (500ml) milk
1/2 cup (110g) caster sugar
1 vanilla bean, split,
seeds scraped
1 gold-strength gelatine leaf*
300ml thickened cream,
lightly whipped

Blueberry compote
1/4 cup (55g) caster sugar
1 cinnamon quill
1/4 cup (60ml) Marsala
(Sicilian fortified wine)
2 x 125g punnets blueberries
1 tsp arrowroot

Place the rice in a saucepan and pour over enough water to cover. Bring to the boil over medium heat, then remove from the heat and drain.

Return the rice to the pan over low heat. Add the milk, sugar, and vanilla pod and seeds, stirring to dissolve the sugar. Cook, stirring occasionally, for 10-15 minutes until the rice is tender.

Meanwhile, soak the gelatine leaf in cold water for 5 minutes to soften. Squeeze out excess water, then add the gelatine leaf to the warm rice mixture, stirring to dissolve. Allow to cool completely, then fold in the whipped cream. Chill for at least 1 hour.

For the blueberry compote, place sugar, cinnamon, Marsala, half the blueberries and 1/4 cup (60ml) water in a saucepan over low heat, stirring until the sugar dissolves. Cook for 1-2 minutes until the blueberries just start to release their juices. Place the arrowroot and 1 tablespoon cold water in a small bowl, stirring to combine, then add to the saucepan with the remaining 125g blueberries. Cook, stirring, for 1 minute or until thickened slightly.

Divide the chilled rice pudding among dishes and serve with the blueberry compote. **Serves 4-6**

* Available from gourmet food shops.

KEY LIME PIE WITH MACADAMIA CRUST

Key lime pie is a classic American dessert that takes its name from the Florida Keys. I've given it an Aussie twist by adding macadamias to the biscuit base.

300g shortbread biscuits
1/3 cup (50g) roasted
　　macadamias
1/2 cup (45g) desiccated
　　coconut
125g unsalted butter, melted
4 eggs, separated
395g can sweetened
　　condensed milk
Finely grated zest
　　and juice of 4 limes
1/4 cup (55g) caster sugar
Icing sugar, melted dark
　　chocolate and raspberries,
　　to serve

Preheat the oven to 180°C and grease a 24cm loose-bottomed tart pan.

Place the biscuits, macadamias and coconut in a food processor and whiz to fine crumbs. Add the butter and pulse a few times to combine. Press the biscuit mixture into the base and sides of the tart pan, then chill for 10 minutes to firm up.

Bake the biscuit base for 10 minutes or until golden, then allow to cool slightly.

Meanwhile, place the egg yolks, condensed milk and lime zest and juice in a bowl and beat with a wooden spoon to combine.

In a separate bowl, beat the eggwhites with electric beaters until frothy. Add the caster sugar, 1 tablespoon at a time, beating constantly until soft peaks form. Fold the eggwhite mixture into the yolk mixture, then pour into the tart case.

Bake for 35 minutes or until the filling is just set. Remove from the oven and cool – the filling will deflate slightly. Chill for 1 hour.

Dust the Key lime pie with icing sugar and drizzle with chocolate. Serve with raspberries. **Serves 6-8**

COEUR A LA CREME WITH STRAWBERRY & SUMAC GRANITA

I've been serving these exquisite cream hearts for years, but recently I've been matching them with a spiced strawberry granita. You can buy the coeur a la creme moulds from kitchenware shops or, alternatively, just tie the mixture up in muslin to form little bundles.

250g cream cheese,
  at room temperature
250g fresh ricotta
1 vanilla bean, split,
  seeds scraped
1/2 cup (75g) icing sugar, sifted
200ml thickened cream
Mint leaves, to serve

Strawberry & sumac granita
500g strawberries,
  plus extra quartered
  strawberries to serve
1 tbs lemon juice
1/2 cup (110g) caster sugar
2 tsp sumac*

Begin this recipe a day ahead.

For the granita, place the strawberries, lemon juice and caster sugar in a food processor and whiz to a smooth puree. Pass through a sieve, pressing down with the back of a spoon to extract as much juice as possible and discarding the solids. Stir in the sumac. Pour into a shallow plastic container, then freeze for 2 hours or until partially frozen. Remove the container from the freezer and break up the crystals by scraping the surface with a fork. Return to the freezer for 1 hour, then remove and scrape crystals again. Repeat this process twice more, then freeze overnight.

Meanwhile, pulse the cream cheese, ricotta, vanilla seeds and icing sugar in a food processor to combine. Add cream and pulse again. Line 4 coeur a la creme moulds with muslin or clean Chux, fill with the ricotta mixture, then fold over muslin to enclose. Place on a wire rack set over a baking tray and chill overnight.

Remove the cremes from the fridge 10 minutes before serving, then unmould onto serving plates. Garnish with mint leaves and extra strawberries, then serve with the granita. **Serves 4**

* Sumac is a lemony Middle Eastern spice available from delis and selected supermarkets.

PISTACHIO CAKE WITH SUGAR-COATED ROSE PETALS

250g unsalted butter, softened
1 cup (220g) caster sugar
1/2 tsp vanilla extract
Finely grated zest of 1 lemon, plus 1 tbs lemon juice
4 eggs
1/3 cup (50g) plain flour
100g almond meal
2/3 cup (100g) pistachio kernels, ground
1 tsp baking powder
1 2/3 cups (250g) icing sugar, sifted

Sugar-coated rose petals

4-6 unsprayed fresh rose petals
1 eggwhite, whisked until frothy
1/3 cup (75g) caster sugar

Preheat the oven to 180°C. Grease and line a 23cm springform cake pan with baking paper.

Place the butter, caster sugar, vanilla and lemon zest in a large bowl and beat with electric beaters until thick and pale. Add the eggs, 1 at a time, beating well after each addition, then fold in the flour, almond meal, ground pistachio, baking powder and a good pinch of salt. Spread into the cake pan.

Bake for 40 minutes or until a skewer inserted into the centre comes out clean. Cool the cake in the pan for 10 minutes, then transfer to a wire rack to cool completely.

Meanwhile, for the sugar-coated rose petals, use a pastry brush to lightly coat the rose petals with the eggwhite, then sprinkle with caster sugar, shaking off any excess. Place on a wire rack and stand at room temperature for 1 hour or until crisp and dry.

Place icing sugar and lemon juice in a bowl. Stir in 2 tablespoons warm water until you have a soft dropping consistency, adding more water if necessary.

Pour the icing over the cooled cake, allowing some to drip down the sides. Serve garnished with the sugar-coated rose petals. **Serves 6-8**

SPRING MENUS

Light and bright

STARTER
Brown rice
& lentil salad

MAIN
Salmon with
spiced carrot sauce

DESSERT
Lavender &
ricotta mousse

192

228

Mediterranean flavours

STARTER
Burrata with
prosciutto and peas

MAIN
Vitello tonnato burgers

DESSERT
Cherry clafoutis

202

216

226

Style on a shoestring

STARTER
Spinach gnudi with sage burnt butter

MAIN
Spring sausage bake

DESSERT
Chilled rice pudding with blueberry compote

196

210

236

204

222

232

Wrap party

STARTER
Bulgogi with easy pickle

MAIN
Crispy fish burritos with salsa criolla

DESSERT
Pineapple carpaccio with sour cream ice cream

EXTRAS

SHORTCRUST PASTRY

1½ cups (225g) plain flour
125g chilled unsalted butter,
  chopped
1 egg yolk

Whiz the flour, butter and a pinch of salt in a food processor to fine crumbs. Add the egg yolk and 2 tablespoons chilled water and whiz until the mixture just comes together. Shape into a ball, enclose in plastic wrap, then chill for 30 minutes before rolling out. The pastry will keep in the freezer for up to 1 month.
Makes one 23cm tart shell, one 30cm x 20cm tart shell or six 12cm tart shells

PARMESAN PASTRY

1½ cups (225g) plain flour
2 tbs finely grated parmesan
125g chilled unsalted butter, chopped
1 egg yolk

Whiz the flour, parmesan, butter and a pinch of salt in a food processor to fine crumbs. Add the egg yolk and 2 tablespoons chilled water and whiz until the mixture just comes together. Shape into a ball, enclose in plastic wrap, then chill for 30 minutes before rolling out. The pastry will keep in the freezer for up to 1 month.
Makes one 23cm tart shell or six 12cm tart shells

SWEET SHORTCRUST PASTRY

1²/₃ cups (250g) plain flour
2 tbs icing sugar
180g chilled unsalted butter, chopped
1 egg yolk
1 vanilla bean, split, seeds scraped

Whiz the flour, sugar and a pinch of salt in a food processor to combine. Add butter and whiz to fine crumbs. Add yolk, vanilla seeds and 1 tablespoon chilled water, then whiz until the mixture just comes together. Shape into a ball, enclose in plastic wrap, then chill for 1 hour before rolling out. The pastry will keep in the freezer for up to 1 month.
Makes one 23cm tart shell, one 36cm x 12cm tart shell or six 10cm tart shells

CHOCOLATE PASTRY

1 cup (150g) plain flour
2 tbs cocoa powder
¹/₃ cup (50g) icing sugar
80g chilled unsalted butter, chopped
1 egg

Whiz flour, cocoa and sugar in a processor to combine. Add butter and whiz to fine crumbs. Add egg and whiz until the mixture just comes together. Shape into a ball, then enclose in plastic wrap. Chill for 30 minutes before rolling out. The pastry will keep in the freezer for up to 1 month. **Makes one 23cm tart shell or six 10cm tart shells**

COCONUT PASTRY

170g plain flour
$2/3$ cup (100g) icing sugar
$2/3$ cup (60g) desiccated coconut
100g chilled unsalted butter, chopped
2 egg yolks
1 vanilla bean, split, seeds scraped

Whiz the flour, icing sugar, coconut and
a pinch of salt in a food processor to
combine. Add the butter and whiz to fine
crumbs. Add the yolks, vanilla seeds and
1 tablespoon chilled water, then whiz until
the mixture just comes together. Shape into
a ball, enclose in plastic wrap, then chill for
30 minutes before rolling out. The pastry
will keep in the freezer for up to 1 month.
**Makes one 23cm tart shell
or six 10cm tart shells**

DULCE DE LECHE

Remove the label from a 395g can
sweetened condensed milk and use a can
opener to make 2 small holes in the top of
the can. Place in a saucepan, pierced-side
up, and add enough water to almost cover.
Bring to the boil, then adjust the heat to
a gentle simmer. Cook for 3 hours, topping
up with boiling water as needed. Remove
the pan from the heat and cool in the water,
then open the can and scoop out the
caramel. Keep the dulce de leche covered
in the fridge for up to 2 weeks. **Makes 395g**

GUACAMOLE

2 avocados, chopped
2 long red or green chillies,
    seeds removed, finely chopped
$1/4$ cup coriander leaves, roughly chopped
1 garlic clove, crushed
1 tbs lime juice
1 tsp ground cumin

Place the avocado, chilli, coriander, garlic,
lime juice and cumin in a food processor
and season with sea salt and freshly ground
black pepper. Whiz until just combined,
but not smooth – you want to keep some
texture. Serve the guacamole immediately.
Serves 4-6

PESTO

2 firmly packed cups basil leaves
$1/3$ cup (50g) pine nuts, toasted
2 garlic cloves, roughly chopped
$1\frac{1}{4}$ cups (100g) finely grated parmesan
150ml extra virgin olive oil,
    plus extra for preserving

Place the basil, pine nuts, garlic and
parmesan in a food processor and whiz
to combine. With the motor running,
add the oil in a slow, steady stream until
a smooth paste, then season with sea salt
and freshly ground black pepper. The pesto
will keep in the fridge, under a thin layer of
oil, for up to 1 week. **Makes $2\frac{1}{2}$ cups**

PLAIN SPONGE CAKE

2 eggs
1/3 cup (75g) caster sugar
1/4 cup (60ml) milk
30g unsalted butter
2/3 cup (100g) self-raising flour
1 1/2 tbs cornflour
1/2 tsp cream of tartar

Preheat the oven to 180°C. Grease and line a 30cm x 20cm lamington pan with baking paper.

Place the eggs in a bowl and beat with electric beaters for 5 minutes or until thick and pale. Gradually add the sugar, 1 tablespoon at a time, beating constantly until combined. Set aside.

Place the milk and butter in a saucepan over low heat, stirring until the butter has melted. Remove from the heat, then set aside to cool slightly.

Sift the self-raising flour, cornflour and cream of tartar into a bowl. Fold half the flour mixture into the egg mixture, then fold in half the cooled milk mixture. Repeat with the remaining flour and milk mixtures, then pour the batter into the prepared lamington pan. Bake for 10-12 minutes until lightly golden and firm to the touch.

Cool the sponge cake in the pan for 5 minutes, then invert onto a wire rack and allow to cool completely. Enclose any leftover sponge cake in plastic wrap and keep in the fridge for up to 3 days or in the freezer for up to 2 months.
Makes one 30cm x 20cm sponge cake

CHOCOLATE SPONGE CAKE

2 eggs
1/3 cup (75g) caster sugar
1/4 cup (60ml) milk
30g unsalted butter
2/3 cup (100g) self-raising flour
1 1/2 tbs cornflour
2 tbs cocoa powder
1/2 tsp cream of tartar

Preheat the oven to 180°C. Grease and line a 30cm x 20cm lamington pan with baking paper.

Place the eggs in a bowl and beat with electric beaters for 5 minutes or until thick and pale. Gradually add the sugar, 1 tablespoon at a time, beating constantly until combined. Set aside.

Place the milk and butter in a saucepan over low heat, stirring until the butter has melted. Remove from the heat, then set aside to cool slightly.

Sift the flours, cocoa and cream of tartar into a bowl. Fold half the flour mixture into the egg mixture, then fold in half the cooled milk mixture. Repeat with the remaining flour and milk mixtures, then pour the batter into the lamington pan. Bake for 10-12 minutes until firm to the touch.

Cool the sponge cake in the pan for 5 minutes, then invert onto a wire rack and allow to cool completely. Enclose any leftover sponge cake in plastic wrap and keep in the fridge for up to 3 days or in the freezer for up to 2 months.
Makes one 30cm x 20cm sponge cake

CUSTARD

5 egg yolks
1/4 cup (55g) caster sugar
2 cups (500ml) pure (thin) cream
1 vanilla bean, split, seeds scraped

Gently whisk the egg yolks and sugar together in a bowl to combine. Set aside.

Place the cream and vanilla pod and seeds in a saucepan over medium heat and bring to just below boiling point. Remove from heat and cool slightly, then whisk the cream mixture into the egg mixture until combined.

Return the custard to a clean saucepan over low heat. Cook for 5-6 minutes, stirring constantly, until thick enough to coat the back of the spoon.

Strain custard into a jug, then cover the surface closely with plastic wrap to prevent a skin from forming. Serve warm or chilled. Keep the custard covered in the fridge for up to 3 days. **Makes 2 1/2 cups**

CLARIFIED BUTTER

Melt 125g unsalted butter in a saucepan over low heat. Bring to a simmer, then cook for 1-2 minutes until foam rises to the top – be careful not to let the butter burn. Remove from the heat and use a spoon to scoop foam from surface and discard. Pass butter through a sieve lined with muslin or a clean Chux, then allow to cool. Clarified butter can be used for sealing pâtés and preserves or for cooking curries. Keep in the fridge for up to 2 weeks. **Makes 1/2 cup**

CURRY BUTTER

2 tsp olive oil
6 eschalots, finely chopped
2 tsp curry powder
1 tbs white wine vinegar
1 tbs tomato kasundi* (optional)
2 tbs chopped coriander
200g unsalted butter, softened

Place oil in a frypan over low heat. Cook the eschalot, stirring, for 1-2 minutes until soft. Add curry powder and cook, stirring, for 30 seconds or until fragrant. Stir in the vinegar and kasundi and cook for 1 minute or until the liquid has evaporated. Cool, then mix well with the coriander and butter.

Spoon onto plastic wrap, then shape into a log and enclose. Freeze until firm. Keep in the freezer for 2 months. **Makes 200g**
* Available from gourmet food shops.

HERB BUTTER

2 tbs chopped flat-leaf parsley leaves
2 tbs chopped oregano leaves
4 anchovy fillets in oil, drained, chopped
2 garlic cloves, crushed
1 tbs lemon juice
200g unsalted butter, softened

Whiz all the ingredients in a food processor to combine. Spoon onto plastic wrap, then shape into a log and enclose. Freeze until firm. Keep in the freezer for 2 months. **Makes 200g**

INDEX

ACKNOWLEDGEMENTS

OUR COOKBOOKS ARE ALWAYS a glorious collaboration of great minds, talented people and a whole lot of love. I'm profoundly aware of the added pressure it puts on our team (yes, we do have to produce a monthly magazine at the same time, too), so my heartfelt thanks goes to the many who have contributed to the end goal.

Firstly, to the team at HarperCollins*Publishers*, especially Shona Martyn and Brigitta Doyle, who have shown such faith in me and offer nothing but kind words and encouragement along the way.

Thanks also to the management team at NewsLifeMedia, who once again gave me the opportunity to create another book under our wonderful *delicious.* brand.

The fact that I work as part of such an accomplished, committed and fun team is something I'm grateful for every day, especially to editor-in-chief Trudi Jenkins for continually believing in me. Also to everyone else at *delicious.*, including managing editor Danielle Oppermann, who continues to be my rock; chief subeditor Shannon Harley, whose cheery smile and talent are an inspiration to everyone; and to Shannon Keogh, Stephanie Westcott and Stephanie Vander Linden, I love you all and thank you for all your hard work.

I'm so lucky to have such a fantastic assistant food editor, Phoebe Wood, whose skills I see develop on a daily basis – thank you for keeping things running smoothly on the magazine while I was busy shooting the book. Also thanks to our new food assistant, Sarah Murphy, who was thrown in the deep end and has taken it all in her stride.

The super-duper design of this book is in no small part due to the combined creativity of two great art directors, Madeleine Kane and Anita Jokovich, who've done a fabulous job of bringing my recipes to life.

Big hugs and kisses go to the incredible team of photographer Ian Wallace and stylist Louise Pickford. It was such a breeze shooting with you at the studio every day (I miss my tea served in a china cup now that I'm back in the office). Thank you both for going that extra mile to make all the shots look so amazing.

A very special thank you to our senior subeditor, Alison Pickel, who took on the role of project editor for the book with her usual diligence and attention to detail, and has made the whole process simple, calm and easy – I can't thank you enough. I truly feel this book is as much yours as it is mine.

Finally, as always, my love and thanks to my family – Phil, Toby and Henry. May we always know the joy of sharing a home-cooked meal.

THANKS TO THE FOLLOWING STOCKISTS

Ici et La Surry Hills (02) 8399 1173, icietla.com.au
Imagine This Woollahra (02) 9327 6713, imagine-this.com.au
Le Grenier online orders, legrenier.com.au
Maison et Jardin Double Bay (02) 9362 8583, maisonetjardin.com.au
Manyara Home Newport (02) 9938 1534, manyarahome.blogspot.com
Ondene Double Bay (02) 9362 1734, ondene.com
Parterre stores nationally, parterre.com.au
Via Rustica Roseville (02) 9416 1113, viarustica.com.au

delicious. uses meat supplied by
Hudson Meats. Visit: hudsonmeats.com.au

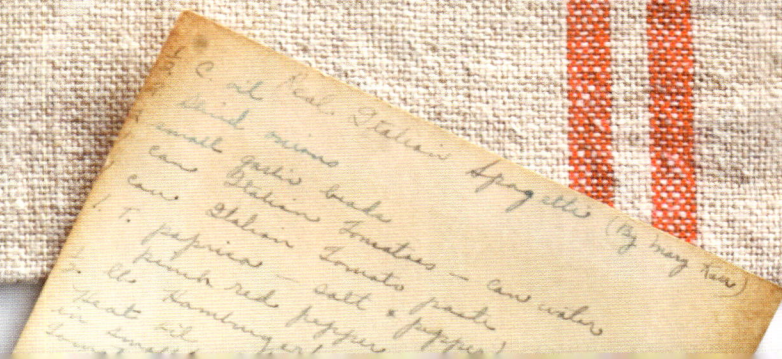

hudson meats

ABC
Books

The ABC 'Wave' device is a trademark of the Australian Broadcasting
Corporation and is used under licence by HarperCollins*Publishers*
Australia. The *delicious.* trademark is used under licence from the
Australian Broadcasting Corporation and NewsLifeMedia.

First published in Australia in November 2012 by HarperCollins*Publishers* Australia Pty Ltd,
ABN 36 009 913 517, harpercollins.com.au

HarperCollins*Publishers* Level 13, 201 Elizabeth Street, Sydney, NSW, 2000, Australia;
31 View Road, Glenfield, Auckland, 0627, NZ; A 53, Sector 57, Noida, UP, India;
77-85 Fulham Palace Road, London, W6 8JB, UK; 2 Bloor Street East, Toronto, Ontario,
M4W 1A8, Canada; 10 East 53rd Street, New York, NY, 10022, USA

National Library of Australia Cataloguing-in-Publication data:
Little, Valli
delicious. Home Cooking / Valli Little
ISBN: 978 0 7333 3134 3 (hbk.)
Includes index
Cooking
641.5

Food Director Valli Little **Photography** Ian Wallace **Styling** Louise Pickford
Art Director Shannon Keogh **Project Art Directors** Anita Jokovich and Madeleine Kane
Managing Editor Danielle Oppermann **Project Editor** Alison Pickel
Chief Subeditor Shannon Harley **Subeditors** Rachel Eldred and Stephanie Vander Linden
Food Preparation Valli Little and Grace Campbell
Assistant Food Editor Phoebe Wood **Junior Food Assistant** Sarah Murphy
Publisher ABC Magazines Liz White **Publishing Editor ABC Magazines** Marija Berem
delicious. **Editor-in-chief** Trudi Jenkins **Managing Director, NewsLifeMedia** Nicole Sheffield

Colour reproduction by Graphic Print Group, Adelaide, SA
Printed and bound in China by RR Donnelley on 157gsm Matt Art

5 4 3 2 1   12 13 14 15

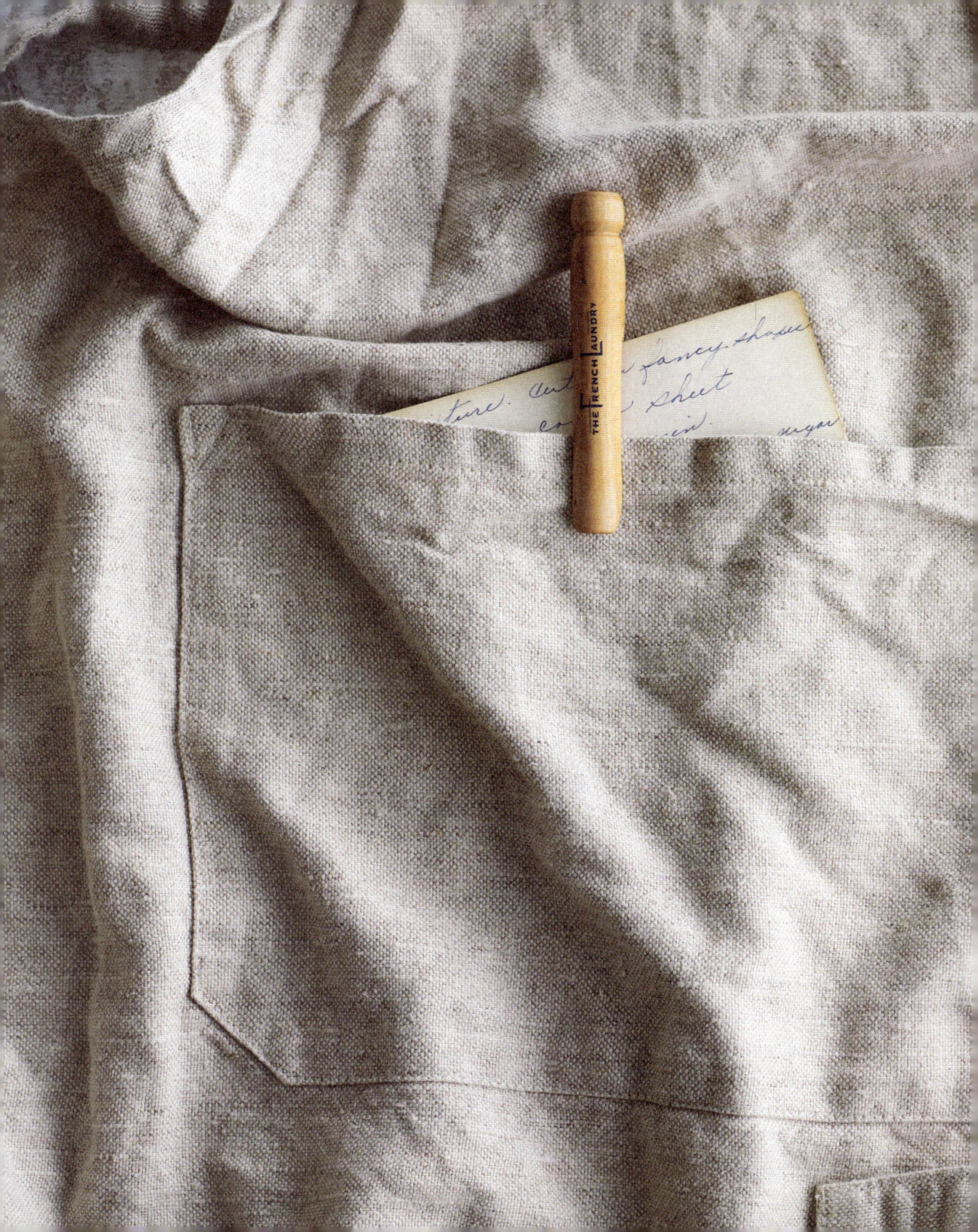
THE FRENCH LAUNDRY